The Dawn of PRO STOCK

Drag Racing's Fastest Doorslammers 1970-1979

Steve Reyes

CarTech®

CarTech®, Inc.
39966 Grand Avenue
North Branch, MN 55056
Phone: 651-277-1200 or 800-551-4754
Fax: 651-277-1203
www.cartechbooks.com

© 2013 by Steve Reyes

All rights reserved. No part of this publication may be reproduced or utilized in any form or by any means, electronic or mechanical, including photocopying, recording, or by any information storage and retrieval system, without prior permission from the Publisher. All text, photographs, and artwork are the property of the Author unless otherwise noted or credited.

The information in this work is true and complete to the best of our knowledge. However, all information is presented without any guarantee on the part of the Author or Publisher, who also disclaim any liability incurred in connection with the use of the information and any implied warranties of merchantability or fitness for a particular purpose. Readers are responsible for taking suitable and appropriate safety measures when performing any of the operations or activities described in this work.

All trademarks, trade names, model names and numbers, and other product designations referred to herein are the property of their respective owners and are used solely for identification purposes. This work is a publication of CarTech, Inc., and has not been licensed, approved, sponsored, or endorsed by any other person or entity. The publisher is not associated with any product, service, or vendor mentioned in this book, and does not endorse the products or services of any vendor mentioned in this book.

Edit by Scott Parkhurst
Layout by Monica Seiberlich

ISBN 978-1-61325-206-2
Item No. CT511P

Library of Congress Cataloging-in-Publication Data

Reyes, Steve.
  The dawn of pro stock : drag racing's fastest doorslammers, 1970-1979 / by Steve Reyes.
    p. cm.
  ISBN 978-1-61325-040-2
1. Automobile racing drivers–United States–Biography. 2. Drag racing–United States–History. 3. Dragsters–United States–History. I. Title.

GV1032.A1R49 2012
796.720922--dc23
[B]

2012019704

Written, edited, and designed in the U.S.A.
Printed in the U.S.A.
10 9 8 7 6 5 4 3 2 1

Front Cover: The legendary match-up between Grumpy Jenkins and Ronnie Sox. A month after I shot the cover photo, the same two cars were racing each other again in Florida, and both of them crashed on the same pass. Larry Lombardo was driving the Vega for Jenkins and he hit a slick spot near mid track. He spun out and tagged the guardrail. Meanwhile, in the other lane, Ronnie Sox' brakes locked up at the finish line, putting him into the guardrail at top speed. Jenkins' Vega was totaled, but the Sox & Martin Duster was repaired. Who says early Pro Stock racing wasn't fun to watch?

Frontispiece: It was no match between "Dyno" Don's Maverick and the Midwest-based Matchmaker at US 131 Dragway in Martin, Michigan. Nicholson and his mighty Maverick raced anywhere and everywhere in the United States, and proved to be Ford's best-running Pro Stock competitor. The image was supplied by Quartermilestones.com.

Title Page: The team of Gapp & Roush has long been associated with Dearborn products even before they joined forces in 1971. Once the duo gelled, it was "look out, world of Pro Stock." Gapp & Roush became a force to reckon with from 1971 to 1975.

Contents Page: This is the 1970 Purple Gang Camaro at Dallas.

Back Cover Photos

Top: The year 1982 dawned with the NHRA's introduction of new Pro Stock rules. Gone were the complex weight breaks, replaced by a simple 500-ci/2,350-pound minimum formula. R/M/S's new big-block program gave them a head start on developing engines for the new generation of Pro Stock. Lee Shepherd ran a 7.86-second ET at the season opener in Pomona, California. It was the first 7-second run in Pro Stock NHRA-style racing.

Middle: Landy's latest Pro Stock car in 1971 was this Dodge Challenger, complete with a 426 Hemi. It was wrenched by brother Mike and featured sponsorship from Edelbrock, Isky, Hooker, Champion, and Stewart Warner. It also had support from Pepsi, Cragar, and Valvoline. The engine was a basic stock Hemi, but the heads were modified to accommodate two spark plugs per cylinder. This concept by Landy helped to make his Pro Stock entry one of the quickest and fastest in 1971.

Bottom: Glidden started his second season in 1980 with his Plymouth Arrow, but when Chrysler filed for a government bailout they ended Glidden's Mopar career. The trusty ol' Fairmont was put back on the racetrack and went head-to-head with Lee Shepherd to retain his championship title.

Author note: Many of the vintage photos in this book are of lower quality. They have been included because of their importance to telling the story.

Contents

Acknowledgments 6
Introduction 6

Chapter 1: Super Stock on Steroids 7

Chapter 2: Pro Stock Originators: The Fab Four 29
   Bill "Grumpy" Jenkins 29
   Sox & Martin 40
   "Dyno" Don Nicholson 49
   "Dandy" Dick Landy 57

Chapter 3: The Competitors 62
   Don "The Okie" Grotheer 62
   Larry "The California Flash" Leal 67
   Wally Booth 71
   Herb "Mr. 4 Speed" McCandless 73
   Melvin Yow 76
   Hubert "The Mouth of the South" Platt 77
   Barrie Poole 80
   Wayne Gapp 81
   Dave Strickler 85
   Don Carlton 87
   Other Movers and Shakers 91

Chapter 4: Trial and Error 101
   Ron Butler 102
   Don Hardy 103
   Speed Research and Development 104
   Wolverine Chassis 106
   M&S Welding 106
   Others 106
   Innovations 110
   Safety Issues 113
   Theft 125

Chapter 5: The Four Horsemen 131
   Bob Glidden 131
   Warren "The Professor" Johnson 139
   Lee Shepherd 147
   Frank Iaconio 151

Afterword 156
Index 157

Dedication

To my three crazy daughters, Ashley, Haley, and Emily. I love you!

Acknowledgments

Thank you to *Drag News, National Dragster, Drag Racing USA, Hot Rod, Car Craft, Popular Hot Rodding*, competitionplus.com, Bret Kepner, Bob Fry, Don Gillespie, Mike Bagnod, Geoff Stunkard, quartermilestones.com, Norman Blake, and John Shanks. Without these publications, websites, historians, and photographers, this book would not have been possible.

Introduction

I must admit, the Pro Stock class was never a favorite of mine. When I first discovered the sport of drag racing in 1963, the Top Fuel dragster was king of the quarter-mile. The only doorslammer class that gained my attention was the Gasser class. Fast forward to 1970. I was a touring drag racing photographer, and the buzz at the 1970 NHRA Winternationals was the debut of the newest Pro class: Pro Stock.

To be honest, I thought the Pro Stock class was a waste of film until I saw some of the driver/owners who raced in the class. Leading the charge in Super Stock were racers Bill Jenkins, Arlen Vanke, and Ronnie Sox. They couldn't wait to go head-to-head against each other in the new class of Pro Stock. The early Funny Car ranks contributed Don Nicholson, Hubert Platt, Dick Landy, and Larry (Butch) Leal, making it a new class definitely worth watching.

For the Pro Stock class to be successful it had to please the paying fans in the stands, but the reaction of the fan base was overwhelmingly in favor of the new style of Pro doorslammers drag racing. They could now root for their favorite car manufacturer—if they drove to the races in a Chevy, they could cheer for the racers driving a Chevy, and the same for Mopar and Ford fans. What a major change for drag racing.

It also gave the manufacturers a new venue for showing off their cars to the public, resulting in greater sales. Let's not forget that competition between the automakers made for a great sport, as well. The Pro Stock class gave the automakers the opportunity to "win on Sunday, sell on Monday." Automakers go by this credo to this day.

In the early years of Pro Stock, I got to work with and know a few stars of the class. One thing I learned quickly was that the little dude they called "Grumpy" really was grumpy! However, if you were straight up with Jenkins, he didn't growl that much. Ronnie Sox was the opposite of Jenkins. Sox was a hardcore racer, but could be found partying with the Top Fuel and Funny Car teams. At Bristol, Tennessee, at a post-race party in 1972, I watched as Funny Car driver Richard Tharpe pulled Ronnie Sox's swim trunks down to his ankles. The crowd around the pool cheered and Ronnie just waved to the crowd, calmly leaned down, and pulled his wayward trunks back up. Ronnie was good people and I miss him to this day. Dick Landy and Butch Leal often crossed my path in NHRA Division 7 World Championship Series (WCS) racing. Both were class act racers. Leal and I did the only Pro Stock fire burnout for a *Drag Racing USA* cover, so yes, Pro Stock racers could get a little crazy too.

As I did the research for this book, I dove deeply into the beginnings of the Pro Stock owners and drivers. It was an eye-opening experience to find out about the skills and determination of these early pioneers of the Pro Stock class. Pro Stock has become one of drag racing's most popular forms of racing and the racers featured in these pages built the foundation that this class rests on today.

The retro A/FX Mopars Jayhawker *and the Candies & Hughes* Jake's Speed Shop *were great examples of what happened to a large part of the Super Stock class in the 1960s. The wheelbases were modified and larger engines with nitro became the norm.*

Chapter One

Super Stock on Steroids

There I was, a fifteen-year-old kid standing at the fence at Fremont Dragstrip in Fremont, California; it was 1963 and I couldn't get enough of those crazy nitro-burning drag cars. The front-engine fuel cars were just too cool. Between rounds of Top Fuel cars, the Stock Cars and Gassers made their attempts at 1320 glory. It was November, so it was a cool day in Northern California, and the crisp air was shattered by the sound of a race car—not just any race car, but a Ford Thunderbolt, a factory race car with Central California's Butch Leal behind the wheel. Leal had Mickey Thompson's new factory racer for just a month and here it was at my racetrack. Butch slammed the gearbox in the Thunderbolt and it was music to any motor head's ears. Now, I hadn't seen many race cars like that at Fremont. It was cool, and different from any other car I had been exposed to. During the next few years, Tommy Grove raced the famed *Melrose Missile* and Butch Leal reappeared with a Mopar Super Stocker.

Once in a while, a young, attractive blond raced her Mopar Super Stocker at Fremont, and that was my first sighting of Shirley Shahan, a.k.a. "Drag-On-Lady." But really, the fastest and most interesting full-bodied racers I saw were the A/FX cars and the Super Stockers. At first it seemed like a class of misfits, with the cars ranging from almost stock to altered wheelbase wonders. Some ran

The Dawn of Pro Stock

Chapter One

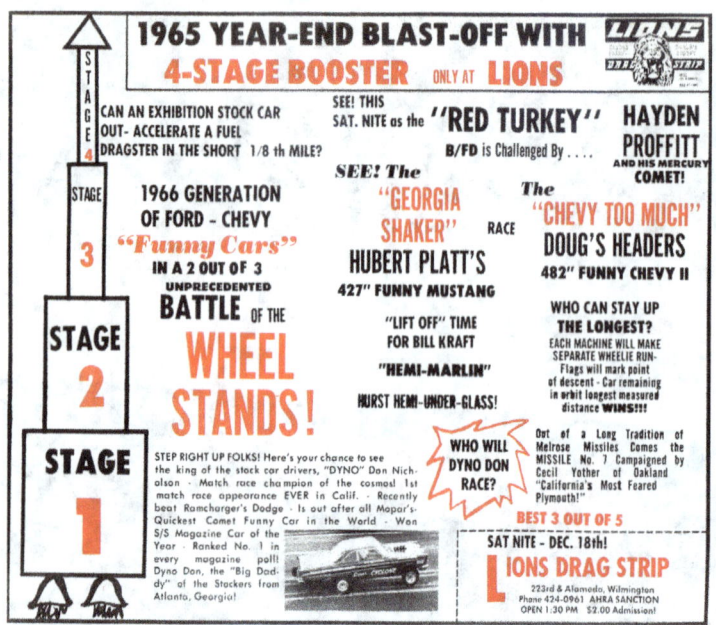

A 1965 *Drag News* ad featured the A/FX cars of "Dyno" Don Nicholson and Hubert Platt at Lions Drag Strip. The West Coast tracks had little respect for the stock-bodied drag racer because the West Coast was the land of the top fuel dragster and many West Coast promoters felt that the A/FX cars were just a passing fad.

Leave it to Fontana track manager, the late Mickey Thompson. He gathered two of the best of the A/FX class to battle at his racetrack. Thompson wanted to see if this stock-bodied, nitro-burning class could fill the seats at the drag strip in 1965.

In this 1965 ad for Irwindale Raceway, "Dyno" Don Nicholson was set to match race the Stone, Woods & Cook AA/GS Willys. The supercharged gas class was king of the stock-bodied race cars on the West Coast. This pairing was rare, and purposely staged to get crowd reaction in a way that enabled the promoters to judge which car the crowd favored.

This was the "Pro Stock" class in 1965. The late Les Ritchey's Ford Mustang was a classic A/FX class race car. It was pure because no extreme body or engine changes had been made, making it a true factory A/FX class car. Ritchey had a huge following of Ford fans, which ended a few months after this photo was taken. Unfortunately, Ritchey was killed while match racing at Fontana, California, which was a huge blow to Ford and its followers. Ford lost its big gun in A/FX West Coast racing.

Early A/FX racing included what seemed like all conceivable body styles as it got started which made for interesting racing. Dave Pinta and Jake Schuliak raced a Ford Falcon pickup truck on the match race circuit with Schuliak at the controls. This thing to cheer about in 1965 racing.

Dave Strickler's loyalty to Chevrolet was put on hold for a few years in the mid 1960s when he traded in his Stovebolt for an altered-wheelbase "bad to the bone" Mopar. Dave did very well in the Dodge, but of course he did well in everything he drove.

In 1965, it was the battle of Northern California versus Southern California. Tommy Grove had vacated his Super Stock Melrose Missile ride for a Ford factory A/FX Mustang. In the other lane was veteran stock-bodied drag racer Les Ritchey and his Ford Mustang A/FX. On this long ago day, Ritchey's Southern California–based Mustang scored a two-of-three victory against Tommy Grove.

Chapter One

Hayden Proffitt was a big star in the stock car ranks in the late 1950s and early 1960s, however he was drawn to the A/FX class and became one of the Mercury backed A/FX stars. He raced for a short time in the A/FX class because in 1967, Proffitt decided to follow the lure of the funny cars and got behind the wheel of a tube chassis Corvair topless funny car.

"Jungle" Jim Liberman was one of the biggest funny car stars of the late 1960s and 1970s and he came out of the stock car ranks. He started out driving an A/Stock automatic Pontiac owned by him and his brother Bob and then took over the wheel of the A/FX Hercules Nova in 1965 to 1966.

nitro and others ran pump gas. It was a lavish blend of Mopar-, Ford-, and Chevrolet-bodied cars. All this chaos soon opened the door for a new class to emerge in 1969, and that was Pro Stock Eliminator. Drag racing was never the same without its factory hot rods.

Drag racing is a sport that is constantly evolving. From the lowest class up to the pro classes, it is an ongoing search for speed and glory on the quarter-mile. The metamorphosis of the Pro Stock class was a strange adventure through many other drag racing classes. No one can argue that stock car classes have always been the backbone of drag racing. The entry fees paid by the "little guy" racer have kept many a racetrack and sanctioning body in business. For example, seventy-five percent of entries in 1965 were stockers. In fact ninety percent of National Hot Rod Association (NHRA) national class records for stock, FX, and modified production stockers were broken in 1965. To say that the Super Stock class was hot in the mid 1960s would be an understatement. Remember, these were the fastest vehicles produced by the manufacturers for public sale.

To qualify for Super Stock competition, a manufacturer had to build a minimum of fifty units. In 1965, only Chrysler Corporation decided to build Super Stock and Super Stock automatics for competition, with 100 Plymouths and 50 Dodges, all with 426 Hemi engines. These racers were also all steel, with lightweight body, chassis, and interior packages. Since the Super Stock class in NHRA was filled with Chrysler products, it was time for a change. Enter the Top Stock Eliminator for NHRA. The hope was to bring all makes and models

Super Stock on Steroids

Ronnie Sox saw a lot of time behind the wheel in the A/FX class. The Sox & Martin *Paper Tiger* altered-wheelbase Mopar was a fan favorite and won a heck of a lot of races for the North Carolina duo. Sox was one of four stock-bodied race car drivers to push for the Pro Stock class. The others were Bill Jenkins, Don Nicholson, and Dick Landy.

The promoters at Half Moon Bay, California, tried something different in 1965 and booked "Dandy" Dick Landy and his *Landy's Dodge* for a special appearance at the scenic dragstrip by the Pacific Ocean. I was there to record the action, but the fans were not amused by Landy's wheel-standing Mopar. The attending crowd could have all fit in one bus. Half Moon Bay race fans were nitro dragster people, not altered-wheelbase Mopar fans.

By late 1966 A/FX stock bodied drag racers started to put people in the stands at Fremont, California. However, the Top Fuel nitro-burning dragster was still king in California.

The Dawn of Pro Stock

Chapter One

Here's Butch Leal in his California Flash *nitro-burning, injected Mopar at Fremont, California, in 1966. A couple years earlier, he piloted a factory Ford Thunderbolt down the quarter-mile.*

Confused? Butch Leal's Plymouth has Super Stock class painted on the side but has A/FX marked on the window in shoe polish. Yes, things would be very confusing until the Pro Stock and Funny Car classes were established.

Although he couldn't race this car at NHRA major events, Landy's long-nose A/FX car ruled the roost in match racing. He won an amazing number of races with this car. When folks started bolting blowers on their A/FX cars, Landy wasn't having any of it because it was getting away from the stock concept and what fans wanted from A/FX racing.

"Just passin' thru" could be the motto for Emmett "Rattlesnake" Austin. He was one of the first stock-bodied A/FX racers to tour the country match racing. Austin had no factory backing, but he could still race with the best. He was based in Alabama.

Like fellow funny car racer "Dyno" Don Nicholson, Edward "Fast Eddie" Schartman tore 'em up in the early Funny Car ranks. Schartman left his Funny Car background for an SOHC-powered Pro Stock Comet in 1971. Schartman didn't have the same success in the Pro Stock ranks and soon faded.

One of a few A/FX drag racers in Northern California, Gene Loflin and his nitro-burning Ford Falcon could be found racing all over NorCal. He would make single runs or race whatever was in the next lane. The guy just loved to race wherever and whenever. Loflin's Falcon was based at his gas/service station in Sunnyvale, California, during the mid 1960s.

Chapter One

The first time the Bakersfield Smokers meet allowed A/FX or any kind of Funny Cars to race was in March of 1967. Here Shirley Shahan is hopelessly outclassed by Bruce Larson and his USA-1 Chevelle. Shahan's A/FX was a super stock with injectors, and Larson's Chevelle was hand built for the early A/FX class.

Butch Leal debuted a shiny new tube chassis nitro injected 'Cuda in 1967 and Leal and his funny 'Cuda quickly became one of the cars to beat in 1967. Here at Fremont, California, Leal puts away the Bloomin' Bullet Camaro.

When the A/FX craze took off in 1967, many super stock racers bolted on injectors and poured nitro in the fuel tank. NorCal's Larry Apodaca went that route with his Penetration Super Stock. Larry learned very quickly that injection and nitro put more horsepower to his now too small rear tires. Every run Larry made was an adventure for him and the fans in the stands. His Super Stock would quickly return to the class it was originally built for and in one piece right side up.

Super Stock on Steroids

After flirting with Mopar race cars for a few years, 1967 saw Dave Strickler in a Strickler-built FX Corvette. However, he hated the way the 'Vette handled down the quarter-mile, so he made it through the 1967 season and took the 'Vette back to his York, Pennsylvania, shop. The 'Vette was stripped and burned to the ground behind his shop. Dave reasoned that he didn't want anyone killed in a car he had built.

"Dyno" Don Nicholson was on top of the 1967 Funny Car world with his Eliminator I funny car. This Logghe Brothers Funny Car was state of the art in early funny cars. Nicholson missed his doorslammer roots and in a few years returned to the racing he loved.

Shirley Shahan became the first woman to win a NHRA major eliminator class in 1965. Two years later, the Central California housewife struggled in the NHRA's C/XS class. The C/XS class was created for stock cars that weren't really true stock. When all was said and done, this class failed to take off and it soon faded away.

The Dawn of Pro Stock

Chapter One

In 1968 Hubert "The Mouth of the South" Platt made a tour appearance in Fremont, California, for Fremont's Annual "King of the Super Stock" Eliminator to battle with Northern California super stocks. Platt was no stranger to Fremont as he had been there in 1966 racing his long-nosed Mustang funny car.

Jim Wetton's Studio Dodge was a very popular Super Stocker in 1968, but Jim drank the A/FX Kool-Aid and modified the Studio Dodge with an altered wheelbase, an injected engine, and nitro to burn. It's too bad, since Wetton's Studio Dodge did well in Super Stock, but not so well as an A/FX car.

the stock car banner. The Top Stock Eliminator was run under an NHRA national record handicap system. The five classes (S/S, S/SA, AA/S, AA/SA, and A/FX) were mixed together under NHRA's new plan, and the official national class records were used for handicap comparison.

Remember the early "Funny Cars," aka A/FX, B/FX, and C/FX? They were now racing stockers in Top Stock Eliminator. The first time these two classes met was at the 1965 NHRA World Championships in Tulsa, Oklahoma. Joe Smith drove the Fenner Tubbs Plymouth S/SA and edged out Bill Lawton's A/FX Mustang for the title. The Super Stock racers still yearned for their own heads-up, single eliminator category. The first sanctioning body to listen to the mounting pressure from the

Continued on page 19

In 1968, Half Moon Bay held its first Super Stock race, and it was obvious that the fans were not interested in this class, as you can see from the spectator stands at race time. To say that the Half Moon Bay fans didn't care for Super Stocks is an understatement.

When the trend for blowers on funny cars came about in 1968, "Dyno" Don Nicholson lead the charge. Nicholson was not a big fan of superchargers as he felt the extra risk of fires and explosions wasn't worth injury or even death. However, he hung in the blower class for the next two years until the birth of the Pro Stock class, NHRA style.

"Fast" Eddie's last fling in Funny Car was his big, bad, blown Cougar Funny Car. Schartman would finish out his Funny Car career in a Cougar and then jump into a factory backed Comet Pro Stock.

Butch Leal's first attempt in Pro Stock was in 1969 when Mickey Thompson recruited Leal to drive his Pro Stock Mustang in the AHRA's new Pro Stock class. Since the Ford Shotgun-powered Mustang had many problems in the engine compartment, this left Leal a first-round runner-up at most races. This rare promo photo was taken by longtime photographer and friend Don Gillespie.

Chapter One

This was the last time Dick Loehr drove his Stampede Mustang funny car because he later sold it and became a factory Ford Pro Stock racer with a new factory Ford Maverick. The Michigan-based Loehr did well for Ford but alas, when Ford cut back, Loehr became one of the victims. Dick took it in stride and turned his attention and effort back to his own business in Kalamazoo, Michigan.

One of the most poplar East Coast A/FX racers was Al Joniec and his Bat Car Ford. Al traded his A/FX Mustang for a series of Pro Stock racers. Joniac raced Maverick and Pinto Pro Stock cars in the early years of the Pro Stock class.

Super Stock on Steroids

stars of the Super Stock class was the American Hot Rod Association (AHRA). Jim Tice and the powers that be at AHRA knew how popular that style of race car was to AHRA sanctioned events. Also, the factory-backed race cars brought more fans and revenue to the association.

Touting a Mopar versus Ford versus Chevrolet battle for supremacy on the quarter-mile could really put AHRA in great standing at the factories, since the manufacturers needed a class to promote their "muscle car" line of street cars. This new "Pro" Super Stock class

Not all of the hard charging early Impalas came from Southern California or from the East Coast. This Chevy sponsored by Alan Green Chevrolet and driven by Dick Milner hailed from Seattle, Washington. Milner raced against the best of the day and was very successful during the early years.

After Joe "Q-Ball" Wale died in the Wale & Candies Top Fuel dragster, Paul Candies regrouped with the Jake's Speed Shop–sponsored Altered Wheelbase A/FX Mopar. This Mopar is a great example of how modified Super Stocks were made in the early A/FX class. Jon Thorne recreated this and the Jayhawker to the smallest detail in the mid 1990s.

The Dawn of Pro Stock   19

Chapter One

was officially added to AHRA in 1969. Super Stock and Stock racers like Bill "Grumpy" Jenkins, Ronnie "Mr. 4 Speed" Sox, "Dandy" Dick Landy, "Akron" Arlen Vanke, "Dyno" Don Nicholson, and a myriad of others now had the Pro Class they had been petitioning for. NHRA saw its popularity and came aboard with the same class in 1970. The manufacturers now had their engineers hit the creative drawing board. The 1320 war was declared for that new Pro Stock Class, and it quickly became the new bloodsport.

Tommy Grove left his very successful Melrose Missile *Super Stock ride for a Ford Factory A/FX Mustang in 1965. Grove did okay in his Ford ride but wanted to go faster and soon he was behind the wheel of a tube chassis nitro-burning Funny Car in 1967.*

Back in the day, Dave Strickler could be found collecting kudos and trophies with his potent Impala. When he wasn't driving his own Chevy, he was out winning behind the wheel of his good friend Bill Jenkins' race car.

Super Stock on Steroids

Dick Brannan's Lively One *Ford Super Stocker is a great example of the true pure Ford Super Stock cars of this era of racing.*

Dick Brannan's Ford Thunderbolt was one of the first dozen given to Ford factory racers all across the United States. The onslaught of these factory racers put Ford in quite a few winner's circles and sent Chevrolet and Chrysler back to the drawing board.

Brannan's Thunderbolt was equipped with a mighty 427 Ford factory engine which was the work horse engine for early Ford drag racers.

The Dawn of Pro Stock

Chapter One

When 1965 rolled around, Gas Ronda had already been a Ford racer for almost five years. In 1965, he was at the wheel of a Ford factory A/FX Mustang. Ronda became Ford's big A/FX West Coast racer after the untimely death of Les Ritchey. Ronda continued racing for Ford until he was badly burned in a Ford factory funny car at Scottsdale, Arizona, in 1970. He recovered from his burns but retired from drag racing.

The Goldfinger Dodge started out as a Super Stock car, but when the Landy's Dodge altered-wheelbase A/FX car began wheelstanding, it started a trend. Marc Danekas "modified" the Goldfinger Dodge, and instead of racing, it became a very ho-hum wheelstander. Thankfully, the Goldfinger soon faded away.

The Super Stock class could be very exciting in the late 1960s, and Sam Hurley showed us just how much fun his SS/AA 'Cuda could be. The spectators loved it.

In 1965, Shirley Shahan was a power company executive, mother of three, a softball star, and a pretty good drag racer. Who says drag racers can't multi-task!

Chapter One

Shirley Shahan and the Drag-On-Lady *put women on the map in early drag racing when she became the first woman to win a major NHRA eliminator at an NHRA national event in 1965.*

Dick Brannan's Lively Too *sort of looked like a* Lively One. *However, they were two very different race cars. The* Lively One *was the legal stock Super Stockers, and the* Lively Too *was Brannan's entry in the newly formed FX/A class, which quickly became the A/FX class.*

Super Stock on Steroids

The multi-car team concept is nothing new in drag racing, and Ed Terry was the other half of Ford's factory A/FX Mustang team. Tommy Grove drove the other black Mustang A/FX. Grove's Mustang was the Charlie Horse, while Terry's was the Quarter Horse. Both cars were based out of Northern California's Hayward Ford dealership stables in Hayward, California, in 1965.

After Tommy Grove left the Melrose Missile team for a Ford factory ride, the Missile was butchered into an altered wheelbased nitro-burning race car. Cecil Yother drove and maintained it for about two years. In 1968, the Northern California team of Sutton & Walls had a Mopar that sported the Melrose Missile name and colors in the Super Stock class. 1968 would be the last of the Melrose Missile race cars.

The Dawn of Pro Stock 25

Chapter One

So, you think it's easy to drive a stock-bodied drag car? They can be a handful, and here the results are in: The score is Guardrail 1, 'Cuda 0.

At Pomona in 1968, two of the best in stock-bodied racing squared off, with Hubert Platt and his factory Ford versus Bill "Grumpy" Jenkins in his Chevrolet Camaro. So, who do you think won? Ford or Chevy?

Super Stock on Steroids

To enter this new drag racing arena, NHRA came up with guidelines and rules for the new Pro Stock Class. The first rules issued by NHRA for Pro Stock in 1970 included:

- Cars had to be American-built with American automobile engines.
- The wheelbase had to be 97 inches or more.
- The body, engine, drivetrain, chassis, etc., could not be altered, modified, or relocated, except as outlined in the class requirements.
- Push starts were not permitted.
- Class was determined by total weight (minimum of 2,700 pounds) divided by the total cubic inches of engine displacement.
- The body had to be a 1968 or later model year of an American factory-produced passenger car.
- Use of fiberglass or other lightweight components was restricted to the hood, front fenders, splash pans, and rear deck lid, but they had to be exact replicas of the stock components they replaced.
- The engine had to be of 1965 or later manufacture, and of the same make as the car.
- Carburetors were limited to two 4-barrels or four 2-barrels and had to be made in America.
- Almost any other internal modifications were permitted.

With these rules, it was time to go Pro Stock Racing!

With all the power and tires available in the stock classes during the 1970s, it could get very dangerous in the hands of a novice driver. Yes, the driver walked away, but the Ford was junk!

The Dawn of Pro Stock

Chapter One

Dick Landy jumped back into the stock classes that he loved in 1967. Landy is seen here from the Riverside Raceway bridge, putting away another foe in Super Stock racing.

*The **Snorkasaurus IV** was a Central California favorite of Mopar fans and it was powered by a Dick Landy research Hemi.*

In a Mopar versus Mopar contest at the 1970 NHRA Spring Nationals in Dallas, Texas, the North Carolina duo of Ronnie Sox and Buddy Martin clashed with Minnesota's John Hagen. This John Steele image captures the action and, a few seconds later, Sox's win light shone and the legendary Sox & Martin 'Cuda continued toward a Pro Stock title.

Chapter Two

Pro Stock Originators: The Fab Four

Because Pro Stock was a new class, there were no clear-cut leaders at the beginning. However, it didn't take long for four names to consistently end up in the final rounds. These four racers—Jenkins, Sox, Nicholson, and Landy—all handled the transition into new territory with relative ease. Their experience and talent truly showed, and they made the most of the opportunity within the new class. The results of their early efforts in Pro Stock contributed to legendary status for each of them.

Bill "Grumpy" Jenkins

The cream always rises to the top, and in the new class of Pro Stock, it rose quickly. Fans of this new class of pro racers quickly latched on to favorites, and the Chevrolet fans' number-one guy was a short, stocky, cigar-chewing Pennsylvania resident named William Tyler Jenkins. Bill Jenkins had been running in organized drag racing for twenty years, and that was saying something since organized drag racing had only been around for

The Dawn of Pro Stock

Chapter Two

"Da Grump" pushed hard for a Pro Stock class in NHRA drag racing and he got his wish, but was caught flatfooted by the factory-backed Pro Stock teams. Even so, he held his own. His early entry into Pro Stock was a converted Super Stocker, but this was soon replaced by a high-tech 1971 Chevy Camaro engineered to compete specifically in Pro Stock. This car was later purchased by Rufus "Brooklyn Heavy" Boyd and raced on the street in the world of Brooklyn street racing. This outstanding photo was shot by Ray Mann and contributed by Quartermilestones.com.

Jenkins put the hurt to an old/new Mopar Super Stock–turned–Pro Stock at Dallas, Texas, in 1970. Jenkins' Camaro was fodder for the early Mopar Pro Stocks, but Sox and company changed all that during the early years. Jon Steele caught this image at the NHRA Spring Nationals.

30   The Dawn of Pro Stock

Pro Stock Originators: The Fab Four

From the files of Quartermilestones.com this is a great image of Bill Jenkins and Dave Strickler's pit area around 1971. Jenkins and Strickler were great friends, and it was a common sight to see the Pennsylvania duo share pit space.

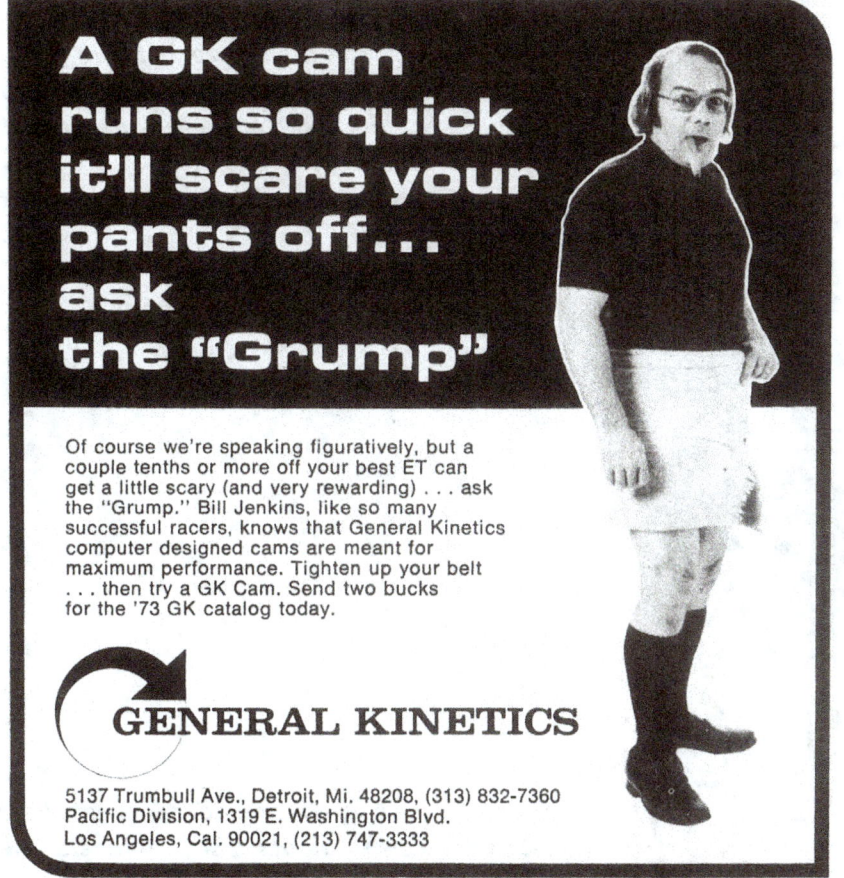

Wanna sell camshafts? How about a nationwide magazine ad featuring "The Grump" with no pants? The aftermarket folks did it all to sell parts and pieces to "Joe Racer," and that spokesperson smiled all the way to the bank.

twenty-two years. He was the brightest star in the Chevrolet battle against Mopar and Ford in Pro Stock. From his 1955 Chevrolet junior stocker to his 1961–1963 *Old Reliable* driven by his buddy Dave Strickler, they won a huge share of races prior to 1966. In 1966, Jenkins brought a 327-powered Chevy II to the racetrack, battled the 426 Hemis all year long, and made the finals, only to lose by red lighting. Remember, back then there were only four major NHRA events run in the United States.

For 1967, Jenkins brought a new 396-powered Camaro to the show, and victory was his at the NHRA U.S. Nationals Super Stock Eliminator. Through 1969, Jenkins terrorized the Mopars and Fords in the Super Stock class. When the new Pro Stock class was introduced in 1970, Bill gained access to Chevrolet's Detroit warehouses for perfectly matched parts and "experimental" items, obtaining lightweight acid-dipped bodies, etc. Then came a 427-ci engine and Jenkins was ready for heads-up Pro Stock racing. The grumpy little guy proceeded to mow down the Mopars and Fords, and then Jenkins kicked off 1970 by beating Ronnie Sox at three consecutive winter races. However, by the end of 1970, the Mopar guys had caught up to "The Grump," so 1971 was a learning experience for Jenkins. He had a good year, but not a great one like 1970. The buzz in the Pro Stock pits was that Jenkins had "lost it," and perhaps his winning combination had disappeared.

Of course, Jenkins didn't care for the "good" 1971 season. Back home in Pennsylvania, "The Grump" went back to building something special for the 1972 Pro Stock wars: an all-new, mini Chevy Vega Pro Stocker. The Pro Stock class was never the

The Dawn of Pro Stock   31

Chapter Two

Under the watchful eye of "The Grump," Larry Lombardo guided Jenkins' new Chevy Monza down the Pomona, California, quarter-mile. Jenkins and Lombardo did well with the Monza, but didn't have the huge (Vega-style) success of the early 1970s. John Shanks shot this photo of the Jenkins team effort.

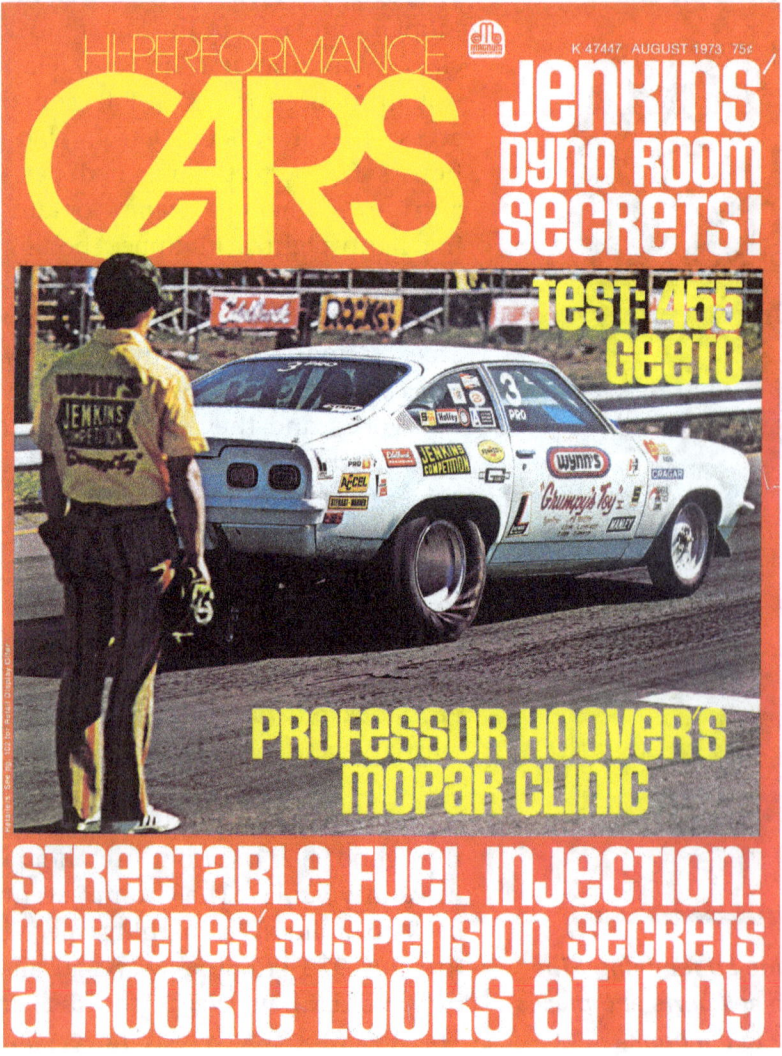

Cars magazine was considered by many to be the East Coast bible for right coast drag racers. They had a great working relationship with Bill Jenkins, who graced many Cars magazine covers, and gave the magazine an exclusive behind-the-scenes look into the workings of his groundbreaking Vega.

The Dawn of Pro Stock

Pro Stock Originators: The Fab Four

same after Jenkins brought his tube-chassis-equipped Vega to the first national event of the NHRA season at the Winternationals. "The Grump" started the 1972 season off right, with an important Pro Stock Eliminator win at the NHRA Winternationals in Pomona, California. He then proceeded to become the first man to win all six of NHRA's National Championship races. He also set a record for NHRA Pro Stock at 9.42 seconds, at 147.63 mph. The Malvern, Pennsylvania, resident gave other Pro Stock competitors something to strive for during the 1973 season.

Bill Jenkins was decidedly one of the most remarkable individuals in drag racing's Pro Stock class. He was an engine builder, driver, and spokesperson for the sport of drag racing, as well as a fan favorite. Yeah, he was a grumpy little guy, but when Jenkins spoke it was well worth writing down. While he didn't say much, when he did it was wise to listen and learn.

Continued on page 40

With the Pro Stock rules changes (which allowed drivers with a small-block wedge engine to run a ligher car), Bill Jenkins' Chevy Vega Pro Stocker was unstoppable. Equipped with Jenkins' innovations and Speed Research & Development's (SRD) super trick chassis, Jenkins' Vega was state of the art in early-1970s Pro Stock racing. Photographer John Shanks' was on hand at Pomona, California, to capture the Vega in action.

William Tyler Jenkins, a.k.a. "The Magician of Malvern (PA)," but to drag fans worldwide he is "Da Grump." He was a trained mechanical engineer from Cornell University and considered one of the founders of the Pro Stock class.

The Dawn of Pro Stock   33

Chapter Two

The only time I was fortunate enough to be at a Jenkins test session was at Orange County International Raceway during the winter of 1972. Of course, I wasn't told ETs or speeds, but I could photograph all I wanted. I think Jenkins made ten runs in about an hour. It almost made you dizzy, how quickly he grouped his runs. Since I was shooting for Wynn's Oil, they got many of the photos from this test session.

To the victor go the spoils at the NHRA Summernationals. Hurstette Shelly Harmon gave Jenkins a victory smooch. Because of Jenkins' small stature, he sometimes needed a step ladder to collect his many victory kisses from the taller race queens.

34 The Dawn of Pro Stock

Pro Stock Originators: The Fab Four

East meets West in the Midwest, when Bill Jenkins got to the finish line first against his left coast foe, Butch Leal, at the 1970 NHRA Indy U.S. Nationals.

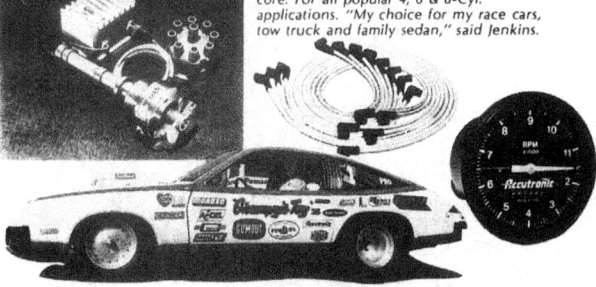

Many aftermarket speed equipment manufacturers turned to the blossoming Pro Stock class for "hero" spokespersons. Bill Jenkins quickly became a Pro Stock superstar and endorsed many aftermarket products, which also put many dollars into his racing bank account.

The Dawn of Pro Stock 35

Chapter Two

It's ironic that one of the forces behind starting the Pro Stock class raced his A/MP Camaro in the first year of NHRA Pro Stock racing. Yes, Bill Jenkins started his Pro Stock career in an A/MP Camaro. He did okay with his makeshift Pro Stock, but realized in mid 1970 that he needed an improvement on the Camaro, so he and long-time pal Dave Strickler debuted an all-new 1970½ Chevy Camaro, and the rest was history. Photographer John Shanks caught this great "Grump" image on film.

Chevy fans, sharpen your crayons. It is time to color your favorite Chevy Pro Stock owner/driver, Bill Jenkins. A page from Tony Collins' Drag Racing Coloring Book *from 1973.*

The Dawn of Pro Stock

Pro Stock Originators: The Fab Four

When the rules changed and Bill Jenkins brought his high-tech Vega into Pro Stock, Don Nicholson was right behind him with his potent Pro Stock Ford Pinto. "Dyno" Don's own Pinto was Ford's answer to the mini Pro Stock rage.

At Pomona in 1972, the fans crowded around Bill Jenkins' all new Grumpy's Toy Vega. Chevy Pro Stock fans expected a lot from "Da Grump's" new Vega, and Jenkins didn't disappoint. Quartermilestones.com provided this photo of the pit action.

Bill Jenkins and his little friend search the Englishtown, New Jersey, pits at the 1980 NHRA Summernationals for the perfect keepsake.

The Dawn of Pro Stock

Chapter Two

"The Grump" spreads "gold dust," and as you can see, Jenkins could handle a broom with the best in the Pro Stock class. He spread the dust, then got in his race car and kicked butt.

Score another Drag News *cover for that grumpy little guy from Malvern, Pennsylvania.*

The Dawn of Pro Stock

Pro Stock Originators: The Fab Four

At the 1973 NHRA Summernationals, "The Grump" squared off with "The California Flash" for all the marbles in Pro Stock. When the win light flashed, the little grumpy dude from Pennsylvania took home the gold.

Jenkins played crime scene investigator at the 1973 NHRA Winternationals as he looked for that "sweet spot" on Pomona's 1320.

The Dawn of Pro Stock

Chapter Two

Sox & Martin

Leading the Mopar nation into the Pro Stock wars was the North Carolina–based duo of Ronnie Sox and Buddy Martin. Sox & Martin have become synonymous with Plymouth through their many victories in the Pro/Super Stock and Factory Experimental ranks. The team formed in 1962 when Martin approached Sox about a partnership. They both had been racing at local North Carolina tracks independently, and Martin was tired of losing to Sox all the time. Both had been racing 409-powered Chevys, with Ronnie racing since 1957 and Buddy since 1958. Their joint effort was an aluminum 427-ci Z-11 Chevy, which was tough enough to turn heads at Ford's Mercury Division. A Mercury factory deal in 1964 was sealed, and the duo became factory racers. They received the first hand-built 427-ci-powered Comet A/FX car and headed for the NHRA Winternationals in Pomona, California, winning the factory Stock Eliminator that weekend.

Ronnie Sox (with the trophy) and Buddy Martin (far left) saw many a winner's circle in 1970. Here, they are joined by NHRA founder Wally Parks. That is crew chief Jake King on the far right.

Photographer Ray Mann shot this great view of the mighty Sox & Martin Pro Stock 'Cuda at Dallas, Texas, in 1970. It was a rolling work of art and muscle car in one winning package.

Pro Stock Originators: The Fab Four

The Sox & Martin Pro Stock juggernaut finished off the NHRA Season in 1970 with a victory at the NHRA SuperNationals in Ontario, California. The North Carolina team was almost unbeatable in 1970 with their Pro Stock 'Cuda. Photographer John Shanks captured this great image of Sox at work.

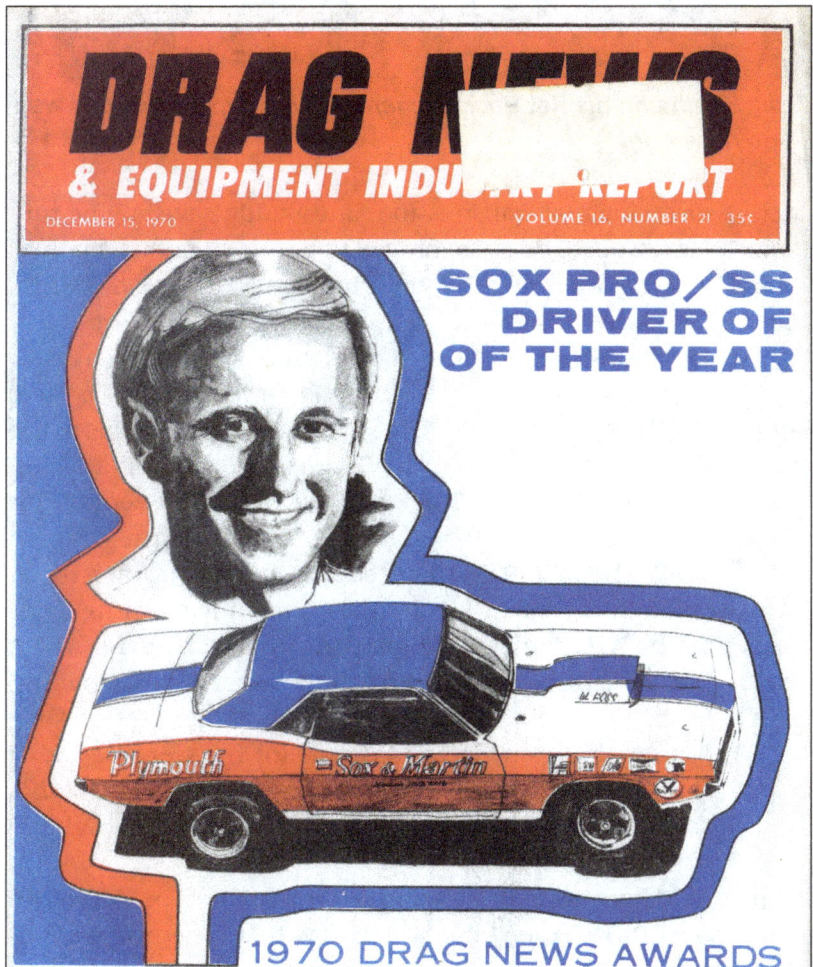

Ronnie Sox's adventures in the Pro Stock class brought him the Drag News Pro Stock Driver of the Year title in 1970, voted on by readers. It was a well-deserved honor for the pride of Burlington, North Carolina.

The Dawn of Pro Stock

Chapter Two

At Dallas, Texas, in 1971 Ronnie Sox said goodbye to Wally Booth and his Rat Pack *Camaro. As you can see, Dallas was one of those tracks where it seemed Sox & Martin could do no wrong.*

So how about match racing? The Comet ran 67 match races and won 62—not too bad a record. The Comet was selected to be on the first U.S. drag racing team sent to the United Kingdom. Upon returning from England, Sox & Martin learned that Mercury was cutting back their drag racing effort, ending their factory support.

The year 1965 was a turning point for the North Carolina racers, as Plymouth had learned of the Mercury cutbacks they quickly moved to put Sox & Martin into Chrysler products for the 1965 season. It was a big year for the Sox & Martin team, as they raced their famed *Paper Tiger*, a Hemi-powered Plymouth Belvedere. That car won 67 out of its 90 races, which isn't the same as 62 out of 67, but was still plenty respectable. Then, in 1966, the team added a nitro-burning Barracuda to their stable of Mopars, but their season was not that exceptional.

At the 1967 NHRA Winternationals, Sox & Martin went back to basics and introduced their Super Car Clinic Program. At their clinic, Ronnie and Buddy explained how their Plymouth race engines and chassis were set up and how to drive against the Christmas tree or flagman starting systems. Sox showed the best way to drive a four-speed manual transmission, and Buddy gave engine tuning lessons. The clinic proved to be a great public relations success, not only for Plymouth but also for Sox & Martin.

The year 1968 turned out to be one heck of a year for the team from Burlington, North Carolina, as they started by winning five out of six Super Stock class races at NHRA, AHRA, and NASCAR Winter Championship events. By year's end, they had added at least another seven major Super Stock wins at national events. This earned Sox the title of AHRA's Driver of the Year. In 1969, the Sox & Martin team went on another terror through the Super Stock ranks, this time winning three major NHRA meets, as well as Top Stock at the AHRA Winternationals; the Mid-South Super Stock Championship in Memphis, Tennessee; the Olympics of Drag Racing at Union Grove, Wisconsin; the *Cars* magazine National Championship at Budds Creek, Maryland; and the U.S. Open Championship in Rockingham, North Carolina.

There was no slowing down for the Sox & Martin gang in 1970, as they started off with a Super Stock Eliminator victory at the AHRA Winternationals running their

Pro Stock Originators: The Fab Four

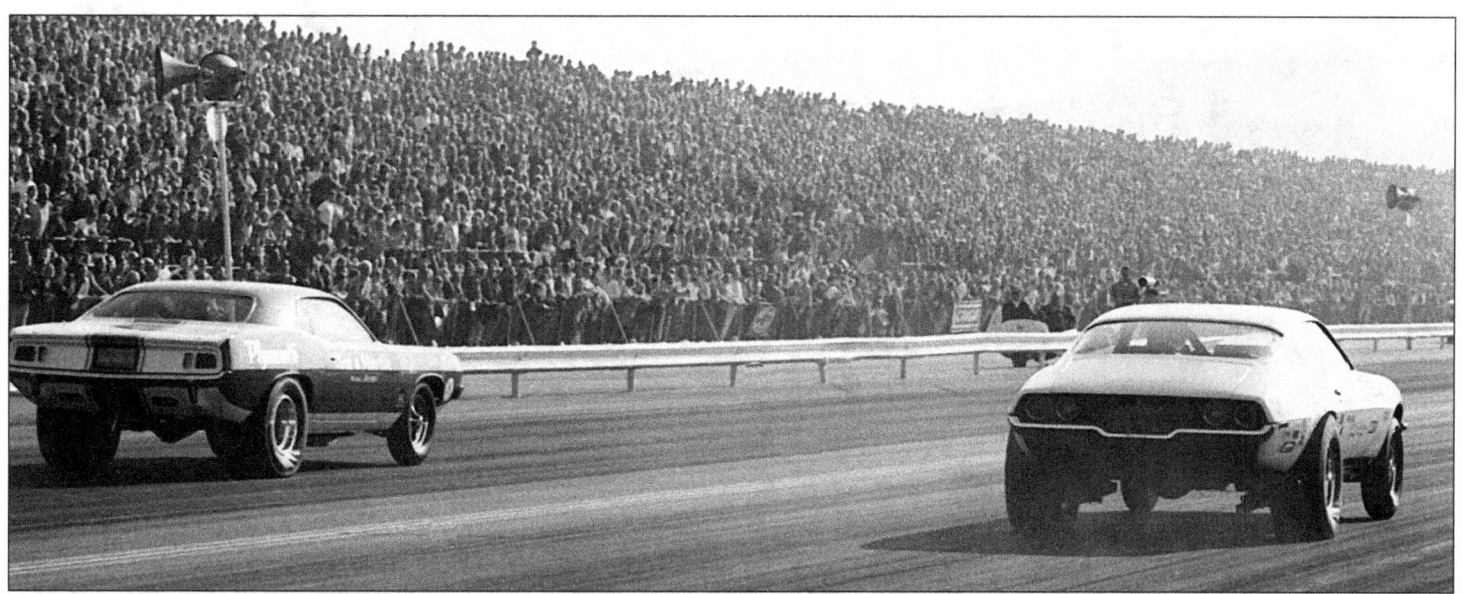

At Englishtown, New Jersey, during the 1971 NHRA Summernationals, a flat rear tire put Sox & Martin on the trailer. Not even a talented driver like Sox could win on three wheels.

The standing-room-only crowd at the 1971 NHRA Winternationals saw Ronnie Sox and Bill Jenkins battle down the 1320, with Sox eventually putting the Pennsylvania-based Jenkins on the trailer. The Sox & Martin versus Bill Jenkins rivalry was one of the most well known in the Pro Stock class. Whether it was at national events or match racing, the rivalry was a Pro Stock fan favorite throughout the United States.

Chapter Two

The Omni was one of the last Pro Stocks that Sox & Martin raced for Chrysler. And while it was one slick piece, it didn't perform up to Sox & Martin's high standards.

A familiar place to find Ronnie Sox in 1971 was in the NHRA winner's circle. Here, Sox celebrates with other winners at the 1971 NHRA Winternationals in Pomona, California.

At the Super Stock reunion in 1996, the dynamic duo of Sox & Martin looked forward to a meet-and-greet of their many fans who attended this Richmond, Virginia, event.

new 'Cuda. The AHRA Super Stock class was the Pro Stock Eliminator in 1970. They ended the year with wins at both NHRA and AHRA World Championship races. Sox & Martin now had the Pro Stock competitors running for the hills. Those boys from North Carolina were serious about their racing, and especially racing in the new Pro Stock Eliminator.

The rampage in Pro Stock was about to begin in 1971 when the Sox & Martin Pro Stock 'Cuda, wrenched by Jake King, collected victories at six NHRA National events and no one could dispute their domination of the Pro Stock class. Of course, this did not sit well with the major sanctioning bodies in drag racing because they wanted to see Chevy and Ford in the winner's circle also. It wouldn't do to bore the Ford and Chevy fans who were tired of seeing a Mopar in the winner's circle. So, the powers that be changed the Pro Stock rules to favor the small-block and wedge-head engines of Chevy and Ford (350 Chevy and 351 Ford).

As all good things must come to an end, the rule changes caused the fortunes of all Hemi-powered Mopar entries to fade, the Sox & Martin team in particular. They had to pack on more weight than the Vegas and Pintos in the class. Wins in 1972–1973 were very hard to come by, so they prepped a 1969 Hemi 'Cuda to race in S/SA for handicap Eliminator and built a new Pro Stock Duster for the 1973–1974 season. Match racing and clinics were their mainstay. Sox & Martin had to be one of the classiest teams in drag racing, and they were just a couple of good ol' boys havin' fun.

From the beginning of the Pro Stock class, when Jenkins raced Sox & Martin, it was a total war on the dragstrip. No other pairing received such a rabid reception. It was the "little" Chevy guy versus the big, nasty, Chrysler Corporation bringing the fans to their feet. This race was a close one, with Jenkins taking the round win.

Chapter Two

Sox & Martin's Plymouth maintained a busy match race schedule, as well as running the national events of NHRA and IHRA. Chrysler's racing chief, Bob Cahill, and then assistant, Dick Maxwell, lovingly refer to Sox as a "trained ape," a human driving machine.

Sox & Martin did have a Colt, and it did race in A/FX after NHRA banned them from Pro Stock. Too many Colts crashed, and one took the life of Pro Stock great Don Carlton. Sox & Martin mainly match raced their Colt on the match racing circuit. I believe Billy Stepp purchased the Colt from Sox & Martin, and Sox drove it for a while.

46 The Dawn of Pro Stock

Pro Stock Originators: The Fab Four

Two of the best face off at the AHRA Winternationals. Sox got the better of Jenkins on this day so very long ago in Scottsdale, Arizona.

The Sox & Martin dynasty began in 1962 and went straight up from there. Plymouth paid the bills, Buddy Martin handled the administrative and managerial details, Jake King built the engines, and when the trio wasn't racing, they ran their Plymouth Super Clinic.

The Dawn of Pro Stock

Chapter Two

David Sox was the younger brother of Ronnie Sox, and one of his perks was getting to shoe the Sox & Martin test car. Aftermarket parts and pieces saw race time on the team's test-mobile.

The team concept was brought full circle by Sox & Martin during their reign in Pro Stock. That cunning duo could spot talent, and Herb McCandless got the call to be the driver of Sox & Martin's team Pro Stock number-two car. McCandless didn't disappoint, and he cleared the way for Sox at many national events. Then, he raced the boss for Pro Stock honors.

48   The Dawn of Pro Stock

"Dyno" Don Nicholson

By the time organized drag racing was established by the NHRA in 1951, twenty-four-year-old Don Nicholson had already experienced drag racing and round-track racing. Fast forward to 1961, and the now thirty-four-year-old Nicholson was piloting his 409-powered Chevy to Top Stock honors at the very first Pomona, California, NHRA Winternationals. Just to prove it wasn't a fluke, Nicholson took his Chevy back to Pomona the next year and won Top Stock honors once again. His back-to-back wins at Pomona not only helped his business in Southern California, but they were also instrumental in his receiving lucrative offers from promoters in the Southeastern United States. So Don packed up the race car and moved to Atlanta to start match racing heavily in the Southeast. Just when things were looking great, Chevrolet dropped its racing sponsorship program. Nicholson was hung out to dry, and his sponsor-less car soon became uncompetitive.

In stepped Mercury in 1964, and Nicholson was again a factory racer. He acquired a bright, shiny, new A/FX Comet, and boy, could that car get down the track. In 1964, he won 90 percent of his races and made the first 10-second run in a doorslammer. In 1965, things got very interesting in the A/FX class as Dodge and Plymouth teams started altering wheelbases for better weight transfer. With better transfer, the car had better traction and ran faster, achieving better times.

Unfortunately, the bigwigs at Ford and Mercury forbade their teams to alter the wheelbases on the

Unlike National Dragster, Drag News *covered all dragstrips nationwide, and "Dyno" Don Nicholson's exploits were splashed on the cover and inside drag racing's "bible" every weekend throughout the racing season.*

It was Ford versus Chevy, and Nicholson versus Zul at the 1975 NHRA U.S. Nationals. "Dyno" Don won a close one against the New York–based Richie Zul and took home the Pro Stock class honors, putting a big smile on the faces of Ford fans nationwide. Photographer Ray Mann caught the action on film.

Chapter Two

Ford fans gathered in the pits of Martin, Michigan's U.S. 131 Dragway to watch "Dyno" Don Nicholson and Earl Wade work on Nicholson's potent Maverick. As always, it was a watch-and-learn lesson for Ford Pro Stock fans. Quartermilestones.com provided this photo of the pit action.

With his success, "Dyno" Don became a spokesperson and pitchman for many aftermarket products. This vintage ad for Auto Meter is a good example.

50   The Dawn of Pro Stock

Pro Stock Originators: The Fab Four

It was no match between "Dyno" Don's Maverick and the Midwest-based Matchmaker *at U.S. 131 Dragway in Martin, Michigan. Nicholson and his mighty Maverick raced anywhere and everywhere in the United States, and proved to be Ford's best-running Pro Stock competitor. The image was supplied by Quartermilestones.com.*

factory-backed A/FXers, and all of a sudden Nicholson couldn't compete against his altered-wheelbase foes. This was not going to fly for Nicholson as he started losing his match race income and his bookings started drying up. In August 1965, Nicholson altered the wheelbase on his Comet, and added injectors to the engine and nitro to the fuel tank. The results were immediate, with Nicholson defeating the much feared Ramcharger's Mopar A/FX. Instead of firing the insubordinate drag racer, Mercury decided to help him go Funny Car racing in 1966.

Mercury had the Logghe Brothers build a tube-framed, one-piece flip-up bodied Comet, powered by a 427-ci Ford SOHC V-8, and "Dyno" Don Nicholson's *Eliminator I* was rarely beat. It ran the first-ever 7-second pass for a funny car in the latter part of 1966. Another banner year for Nicholson and his *Eliminator 2* was 1967, until other funny car teams bolted superchargers on top of their engines. Nicholson followed suit with a blower on his car, and the race was on. In 1968, Don debuted a new supercharged Cougar-bodied funny car at the NHRA Winternationals. The Nicholson dynasty took some heavy blows all throughout that year, with blower explosions, funny car fires (including one that burned the car to the ground), and the ultimate, a lightning strike that burned his Atlanta shop to the ground.

After such a dismal year, he jumped to Super Stock match racing, only to hear whispers that a new class for 9-second stockers was about to be announced. Pro Stock was coming to drag racing. Ford signed Nicholson to pilot a Maverick in the new class for 1970. Ford gave him a whole seven days to get his Pro Stock prepared for its

"Dyno" Don Nicholson's Maverick was built by the Azusa, California–based M&S Welding shop in seven days. It proved to be time well spent, as the Maverick quickly rose to the head of the Pro Stock class. Nicholson earned Ford's first national victory in the newly formed Pro Stock class. Ace photographer John Shanks captured "Dyno's" Maverick smokin' the tires at Ontario, California.

The Dawn of Pro Stock

Chapter Two

debut at the NHRA Winternationals. While he didn't win, Nicholson had made an appearance and put everyone on notice that he was back. Nicholson and his longtime engine tuner Earl Wade made some adjustments and took the Maverick on tour where they dominated everywhere they raced. At one point while on tour, the duo won 45 straight rounds of drag racing and Nicholson gave Ford its first NHRA Pro Stock win with a victory at the 1971 Summernationals.

At the beginning of the 1972 season, Nicholson exchanged his SOHC-powered Maverick for a Pinto with a 351 Cleveland engine and had a decent year. The following year proved to be even better for the team of Nicholson and Wade as they scored wins at three consecutive nationals events, including the AHRA Winternationals (at Scottsdale, Arizona), the NHRA Winternationals (at Pomona, California), and the NHRA Gatornationals (at Gainesville, Florida).

After competing in the major NHRA and AHRA events in 1973, Nicholson began running more match races all across the United States. He had a huge fan base, and this was the best way to make money and see the fans who had supported him throughout his drag racing career. In 1977, Nicholson decided to race all of NHRA's major events—something he hadn't done since his breakout 1973 Pro Stock season. It didn't take long before Nicholson was in the NHRA Pro Stock winner's circle at the 1977 NHRA Gatornationals, Spring Nationals, and U.S. Nationals. He was crowned the Winston NHRA Pro Stock Champion for 1977, which proved to be the pinnacle year of his career.

"Dyno" Don Nicholson made another attempt at becoming NHRA's World Pro Stock Champion in 1979 but finished third. So when Ford called it quits in 1980, Don retired for about four years until he couldn't take it anymore.

He found an Oldsmobile to go Pro Stock racing with in 1984. The partnership with Oldsmobile never did gel, and from 1988 to 1991 Nicholson was found touring his 409 Impala at Super Chevy shows and match races all around the country. When all was said and done, Nicholson figured he had traveled more than 1,400,000 miles and spent

Two of the best in the early years of Pro Stock went head to head at Pomona in 1971, with "Akron" Arlen Vanke edging out "Dyno" Don Nicholson at the finish line. Vanke and Nicholson faced each other many times in the early years of Pro Stock racing.

every dollar he had ever earned on racing. He had raced the greatest Funny Car, A/FX, Stock, and Pro Stock cars ever to grace the quarter-mile, and he had beaten them. In fact, he is the only racer to make final rounds in six different NHRA classes, including Funny Car, Pro Stock, Super and Comp Eliminator, Stock, and Street.

Before I close this segment, many will want to know about "Dyno" Don's nickname. Nicholson's version is that it was given to him by a track announcer while match racing down South. Another version is that he ran a dyno while working at his brother's automotive shop. I leave it to you to choose the version that appeals to you.

It was the wiley old veteran versus the high-tech guys at Gainesville, Florida, and Nicholson drew on his vast racing knowledge to pull out a victory against Don Carlton and the Motown Missile *gang. Those Michigan-based Motown boys were serving notice to the Pro Stock guys that they were a real threat on the quarter-mile.*

Ford Maverick, Ford Pinto, or Ford Mustang, "Dyno" Don Nicholson made them all winners on the national or match race circuit. You can say that Nicholson put Ford on the map when it came to Pro Stock.

The Dawn of Pro Stock

Chapter Two

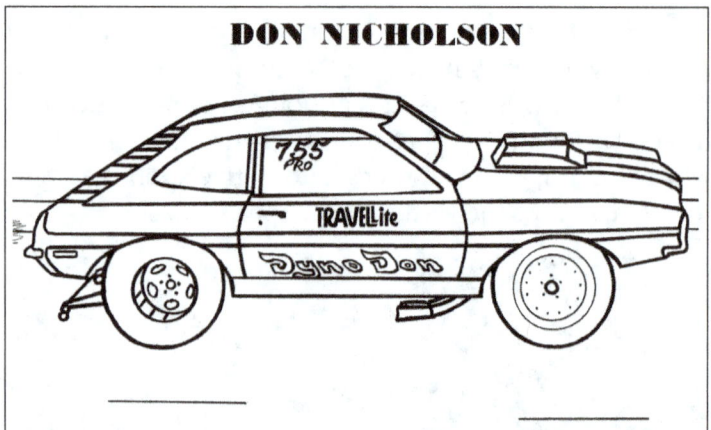

If you had a Tony Collins' Drag Racing Coloring Book, *you could add some color to "Dyno" Don and his mighty Ford Pinto Pro Stock.*

Would you buy a carburetor from these guys? Holley thought the public would, and used Jenkins, Booth, and Nicholson as spokespersons and salesmen in 1970.

It was "Dyno" Don's Pro Stock Pinto, but it wasn't "Dyno" Don behind the wheel. With all the multiple bookings, a second "Dyno" Don Pinto was put out on the match race circuit. Veteran driver Ken Dondero was at the wheel of Nicholson's number-two car. Dondero had such great success with Nicholson that he went on to drive match race Pro Stockers for Bill Jenkins and Gapp & Roush, which wasn't bad for a resume.

54   The Dawn of Pro Stock

Pro Stock Originators: The Fab Four

A ritual all the early Pro Stock racers were familiar with was the spreading of "gold dust," or rosin. In this photo, "Dyno" Don Nicholson applies the dust to the York US 30 Dragway surface. The rosin put more bite to the rear wheels if applied correctly. Putting down the rosin was very much an art form in those days, and most drivers did their own spreading of the dust.

In 1963, when Chevy dropped their factory backing program, Nicholson made the jump to a Mercury Comet for the 1964 season. His A/FX racer won 90-percent of its match races and made the first-ever 10-second run in a doorslammer class.

The Dawn of Pro Stock

Chapter Two

In 1972, Nicholson switched to a 351 Cleveland-powered Ford Pinto. He then started the 1973 season by winning three national events in a row, including the AHRA Winternationals, NHRA Winternationals, and the NHRA Gatornationals.

When Ford cut back in 1980, Nicholson went into retirement. But Oldsmobile offered him a deal in 1984, and he jumped at the chance to race Pro Stock again. However, "Dyno" Don didn't burn up the Pro Stock world and soon faded from the class.

"Dyno" Don Nicholson was one of the most popular drag racers to go down the quarter-mile. He even had his own fan club.

56   The Dawn of Pro Stock

Pro Stock Originators: The Fab Four

"Dandy" Dick Landy

All week long, the local radio station had been promoting an appearance by the *Landy's Dodge* at Half Moon Bay dragstrip. Of course, I had heard of Landy, but I had never seen the Dodge. And, to be honest, I was really at Half Moon Bay for the two-out-of-three match race between "Big" John Mazmanian's candy red 1941 Willys AA/GS and Stone, Woods, & Cook's pearl-blue 1941 Willys AA/GS. However, there in the staging lanes was a rather stock-looking gray, almost silver, Mopar with injector stacks poking through the hood. Landy cleaned out the raspy Mopar engine and staged. The start light went green and the Dodge leap-frogged from the starting line with its front wheels high and nose pointed skyward as it headed for the finish line. No, I was not impressed.

Fast forward to late 1966. We were at Fremont Dragstrip's big A/FX bash, and there was Dick Landy's Dodge again. It was longer and lower, and without the silly wheelstands when it ran. Now this could be a real race car. Landy proceeded to win 90 percent of his races with his long-nose injected Dodge that year, and for a guy who started drag racing in the late 1950s and early 1960s with his dad's Ford pickup truck, he had come a long way. Dodge saw the raw talent of Dick Landy and signed him up in 1963. This made Dick Landy's name synonymous with Chrysler and Mopar performance for more than forty years.

Landy was one of drag racing's first "factory" drivers. He drove a 413-powered Max Wedge Plymouth to the dismay of fellow racers, and then switched to a 426-ci Wedge Dodge for the 1964 season. After that, he

"Dandy" Dick Landy's Mopar was a welcome addition to any racetrack's pit area. His colorful rig attracted Mopar fans like a moth to a light bulb. To say Landy was popular would be a huge understatement. Quartermilestones.com supplied this image.

Two of the early powerhouse Mopar teams square off at Englishtown, New Jersey: Californian Dick Landy versus Mike Fons driving The Rod Shop *Mopar. Landy could be found racing everywhere in the United States, and was one of the first to conduct nationwide Dodge Performance clinics.*

The Dawn of Pro Stock

Chapter Two

This hard-working gentleman is Mike Landy, Dick Landy's brother and right-hand man. Mike was the unsung hero in brother Dick's racing effort. This is another pit action image supplied by Quartermilestones.com.

In 1982, Dick Landy dispensed advice to Butch Leal on Pomona's starting line. Landy had no problem sharing his vast knowledge of Pro Stock with anyone who asked for his help.

"Dandy" Dick Landy started his Pro Stock career with his first major victory on May 17, 1970, at the first annual Colorado Pro Stock Championships at Continental Divide Raceway in Castle Rock, Colorado. Landy defeated Bill Bagshaw to capture top Pro Stock honors. John Shanks clicked this photo at Bakersfield, California.

Pro Stock Originators: The Fab Four

entered the altered-wheelbase A/FX class with one of his most famous race cars, the Hemi-powered *Landy's Dodge*. In 1965, Landy was racing one of the twelve altered-wheelbase A/FX cars built by Chrysler (six by Dodge and six by Plymouth). When it wasn't clawing at the sky, it ran in the low-9-second range at 140 mph. The long-nosed car I had seen at Fremont could only run match races, as it wasn't allowed to race at NHRA events. This didn't stop Landy from a very lucrative match race career. And the fans loved the flamboyant, cigar-chomping driver from California.

When 1967 rolled around, Chrysler had something new in store for their star West Coast–based drag racer. They asked him to conduct performance seminars at Dodge dealerships across the United States. Now that A/FX cars were turning into funny cars full of nitro and superchargers, Landy felt this moved away from his (and Dodge's) fan and customer base. Both Landy and the Dodge brass agreed that Landy should race a stock-bodied, stock-class race car, so along with good friend Bob Lambeck, and with the help of his brother Mike, a new *Landy's Dodge* Super Stocker hit the quarter-mile.

In 1970, the Pro Stock class was in full swing, and Lambeck had left Landy to race his own S/S/Pro Stock

Get your crayons ready. "Dandy" Dick was one of the Pro Stock racers featured in Tony Collins' Drag Racing Coloring Book in 1973.

Landy's Dodge was one of twelve (six Plymouths and six Dodges) built by the Chrysler Corporation with its wheelbase altered. Its design signaled the beginning of quicker and faster times for these early "funny cars." When Landy wasn't playing wheelstander, the Dodge ran in the low 9-second range at more than 140 mph, which was very impressive for that time period.

The Dawn of Pro Stock

Chapter Two

Mopar. With the help of his Chrysler sponsors, Landy assembled his first Pro Stock Dodge and quickly raced to victory. He waded through a killer sixteen-car field to defeat Bill Bagshaw at the Continental Divide Raceway in Castle Rock, Colorado. The event was the first annual Colorado Pro Stock Championship on May 17, 1970.

"Dandy" Dick continued to be a big asset for Chrysler as he raced and spoke at performance clinics around the country during the next ten years. He also remained competitive during his tenure in the Pro Stock class, winning the AHRA Pro Stock Championship in 1973 and 1974. A bit of trivia on "Dandy" Dick: He didn't smoke, yet went through fifty-six boxes of cigars a year. Why a cigar? When Landy drove for Andy Andrews early in his career, Andrews handed him a cigar each time he got in the race car for good luck. I would say that drag racing was lucky to have "Dandy" Dick Landy.

I believe this was one of the classiest ads ever done featuring the Fab Four in Pro Stock. The style is unmistakably that of Al Hirschfeld, noted illustrator and artist to the movie stars, making this ad one of a kind.

Landy's latest Pro Stock car in 1971 was this Dodge Challenger, complete with a 426 Hemi. It was wrenched by brother Mike and featured sponsorship from Edelbrock, Isky, Hooker, Champion, and Stewart Warner. It also had support from Pepsi, Cragar, and Valvoline. The engine was a basic stock Hemi, but the heads were modified to accommodate two spark plugs per cylinder. This concept by Landy helped to make his Pro Stock entry one of the quickest and fastest in 1971.

Dick Landy was always easy to spot at any racetrack. The larger-than-life Landy always had a cigar clinched in his pearly white teeth. Landy once said that he went through fifty-six boxes of cigars a year, yet he never smoked one.

The Dawn of Pro Stock

Pro Stock Originators: The Fab Four

One of Dick Landy's last major national Pro Stock wins came at the AHRA-sanctioned Beeline Dragway in Scottsdale, Arizona. Landy then vacated the driver's seat and let Paul Genilozzi and Brad Yuill drive his mighty Mopar.

In 1973, Dick Landy and Butch Leal were still carrying out their eight-year rivalry that started in 1965 while in the A/FX class. Landy's and Leal's A/FX cars went head to head at Southern California's racetracks during the winter months when the two were off their tour and match race duties.

The Dawn of Pro Stock

"The Mouth of the South," Hubert Platt, really gave Ford fans something to cheer about in the early 1970s. The always colorful Platt delighted fans with wheels-up launches and smoke-filled burnouts. This photo was supplied by Quartermilestones.com.

Chapter Three

The Competitors

Beyond the big guns, there were plenty of other racers who also had the potential to win at any given event. Running similar equipment and possessing similar levels of experience, they forced the top-tier teams to always be at their best. This group of early Pro Stock competitors may not have enjoyed the same level of success as the quartet of Pro Stock legends in Chapter Two, but they certainly were worthy competitors who worked just as hard, traveled just as far, and entertained just as much.

Don "The Okie" Grotheer

With the battle of the manufacturers really heating up in the Pro Stock class, the early years produced some big-time fan favorites. One of them was Don Grotheer of Cushing, Oklahoma, who had started out street racing a 1950 Ford when he was just sixteen years old. Later, his 1957 Chevy 150 business sedan (with a 245-hp, 283-ci Power Pack V-8) was the first of four 1957 Chevys he raced between 1957 and 1960. Don took home his first

62   The Dawn of Pro Stock

The Competitors

Don Grotheer started his drag racing career in 1958, and then, in the 1971 NHRA Winternationals, he wheeled a Mopar-backed 'Cuda in the Pro Stock class. Grotheer was chosen to be one of the elite Mopar racers to put on Plymouth Supercar clinics nationwide in 1969. He continued to do so throughout the 1972 season. This photo was captured by John Shanks at the 1971 NHRA Winternationals.

"The Okie" versus "The Grump" at Columbus, Ohio, in 1972, where Grotheer and Jenkins clashed many times in early NHRA Pro Stock racing. This time they were paired at the NHRA Spring Nationals, and Grotheer couldn't stop Jenkins' march to winning Pro Stock Eliminator.

real drag race trophy at Oklahoma City's JC's dragstrip around 1958. Then, in 1963, Don found himself at the wheel of his own 426 Stage 1 Max Wedge Plymouth, made available to him by Don's good friend and new-car dealer Tom Sparks. Sparks had taken delivery of two Max Wedge Plymouths, one an automatic and one a three-speed stick, which Don purchased and raced. He updated his racer to a stage-two Max Wedge and cruised to an AHRA Top Stock Championship and an NHRA Central Division Top Stock Points Championship.

Around 1965, Chrysler started to take notice of this "Okie" in Top Stock, and late in the year Chrysler offered Grotheer one of its new street Hemis. The deal was simple: Purchase the car and Chrysler would supply all those really cool factory parts and pieces. So he purchased a 1966 Plymouth Belvedere street Hemi and readied it for its debut at the 1966 NHRA Winternationals in Pomona, California, where he put Bill Jenkins' *Chevy II* on the trailer to win the class. However, a red light against Shirley Shahan spelled the end of his quest for Stock Eliminator at that event.

Don and his mighty Belvedere raced all of the NHRA national and Division 4 events, bringing home the 1966 NHRA Division 4 Championship. This made both Don and Chrysler very happy. The following year, Don repeated his record with a new car and another NHRA Division 4 Championship. In 1968, Chrysler stepped up with a Hurst Hemi 'Cuda Super Stocker for the young man from Oklahoma. Don had a great time in his 'Cuda, setting many NHRA SS/B and SS/BA records wherever it raced.

The Dawn of Pro Stock 63

Chapter Three

In a battle of the Mopars at the 1972 NHRA Winternationals, Don Grotheer narrowly defeated fellow Mopar racer "Akron" Arlen Vanke in his race for the win. He went on to become runner-up to Bill Jenkins' dominant Chevy Vega.

Don Grotheer earned a spot on the Plymouth Supercar Clinic program because of the demand by Chrysler-Plymouth dealers for clinics at their dealerships. Being well spoken and personable, "The Okie" fit well as a spokesperson for Mopar.

The Dawn of Pro Stock

The Competitors

After being dumped by Chrysler in early 1973, Don Grotheer built a Don Hardy–chassis'd Ford Pinto, which he debuted at the NHRA U.S. Nationals. He then proceeded to outperform all the remaining Mopar-backed Pro Stock cars. Grotheer went to the semi-finals at Indy, but was still without a sponsor after his strong performance. Grotheer then sold his Pinto and walked away from drag racing.

Don Grotheer found out about the rosin bite at the famed Lions Drag Strip in 1971. Grotheer's bent front end made him think about wheelie bars for his Oklahoma-based 'Cuda.

The Dawn of Pro Stock

Chapter Three

The next year, the gang at Chrysler had big plans for Grotheer. Sox & Martin were swamped between racing and holding their clinics. Chrysler/Plymouth dealers were stepping all over themselves to get a clinic at their dealerships. So, Chrysler added Grotheer to their roster of clinic instructors. It was a tough grind, but with the help of Dick Maxwell (boss), Jerry Mallicoat (PR), and Joe Smith (assistant and go-to guy), Grotheer put on three or four clinics a week, with the last one in close vicinity to the next race. From 1969 to 1971, Don taught seventy-five clinics each year.

When Pro Stock came on the scene, Grotheer explored it as an option. Being a sheet-metal worker by trade, Don knew his way around metal, and in 1970 built his first Pro Stocker with some help from Chrysler. The 1970 'Cuda was built right in Grotheer's shop. After learning the ropes in Pro Stock racing, he had Don Hardy build his Pro Stock entry for the 1971 season. In addition to that car, Grotheer also raced a 1971 Hemi Road Runner in B/MP. Both cars proved to be winners, with the Pro Stock car setting the top mile-per-hour record at its first race, the NHRA Gator nationals. The B/MP car (with Butch Leal driving) won its class at Pomona, and Butch also won the GT1 class at the AHRA Winternationals at Beeline Drag Way in Scottsdale, Arizona. The B/MP car (with Don at the controls) won every race it entered, including the Modified Eliminator at the NHRA Summernationals.

However, all good times must come to an end. When NHRA decided to play games with the Pro Stock rules, putting so many restrictions on the Chrysler products to "even the playing field," it was a game changer. So, in 1973, Grotheer built his last Pro Stocker, a Ford Pinto, which debuted at the NHRA U.S. Nationals in 1973. Don out-qualified all the Chrysler Pro Stockers and went on to the semi-final round. But the Pinto was all Don, with no factory support, and with no sponsors in sight Don sold the Pinto and retired from the sport he loved, to spend more time at his business and with his wife Joann and their two sons.

Tough and independent was the only way to describe Jim Hayter. His Camaro gave the factory Pro Stock racers major headaches. He was one of two Pro Stock racers to emerge from the small Oklahoma town of Cushing, with the other being Don Grotheer.

Besides racing his Pro Stock 'Cuda in 1971, Grotheer also raced a B/MP Plymouth Road Runner. At the beginning of 1971, good friend Butch Leal was at the wheel driving the Road Runner to a victory in class at Pomona, California, and Scottsdale, Arizona. Then Grotheer took over the driving for 1971 and won every AHRA GT1 Eliminator, the B/MP class, and Modified Eliminator at the NHRA Summernationals. Grotheer also set the B/MP record at 10.46 seconds.

The Competitors

Larry "The California Flash" Leal

Out of Pixley, California, in 1960 came a fresh-faced Larry (Butch) Leal, who decided that drag racing, not farm chores, was in his future. The sixteen-year-old convinced his dad to purchase a new El Camino for him to race, and he started attending the drag races not far from home at Bakersfield, California. Consistent wins and super-fast times were quickly associated with young Leal as he continued impressing race fans. In 1962, Butch built his first Chevy Super Stocker with a 409-ci engine. But Leal needed to go faster, so in early 1963 he started driving his 427 Z-11-powered Chevy, which was an engine package only a chosen few had received from Chevrolet. However, mid-season in 1963, Butch had a "better idea" and changed out his car for a Ford Galaxie with a 427-ci engine.

Butch terrorized the Super Stock class with his Ford Galaxie, and in 1964 he traded it for a shiny new Ford, one of eleven factory-built Thunderbolts. This was the first car I saw him drive at Fremont, California, and it was cool to watch Butch slam through the gears of that Fairlane Thunderbolt. However, never one to get stuck in a rut, Butch moved on in 1965, becoming a Mopar factory racer and building two race cars for Plymouth: an altered-wheelbase car and a stock Plymouth Belvedere. He did very well in both. His race winnings in 1965 totaled more than $96,000, so Butch relaxed a little with his second love, golf, for the entire 1966 season. In 1967, relaxed and ready to race, Butch entered the world of funny car racing.

Leal's 1967 season started with a nitro-burning, injected 'Cuda, painted in what was now his trademark orange and white colors. In the blink of an eye, Leal's 'Cuda was the quickest and fastest injected funny car in the United States. When 1968 rolled around, you'd think Butch would be ready to bolt on a blower with his soon-to-be-delivered new Logghe Brothers-built 'Cuda, but he was not. Butch liked Don Nicholson and

Butch Leal went head-first into the A/Fuel Funny Car class in 1967 with his injected and tube-chassis-equipped 'Cuda, the quickest and fastest of the nitro-burning injected funny cars in the country. When the 1968 season began, Leal's 'Cuda was nowhere to be found. He had abandoned the dangerous Funny Car class for Super Stock, and golf.

Butch Leal vacated his Mickey Thompson Pro Stock ride and debuted a Chevy Camaro-based Pro Stock car early in 1970. Leal had some success with his Camaro, but breakage problems sidelined him throughout 1970. Here at Bakersfield, California, Butch put Darrell Droke's Darrell & Darrell Pro Stock Maverick on the trailer at an NHRA WCS Division 7 event.

Chapter Three

Butch Leal's Pro Stock Camaro was a very slick race car, but breakage woes led to him foregoing his Stovebolt for a Mopar in 1971. Butch sold his Camaro at the end of 1970 to fellow Pro Stock racer Rufus Boyd, a.k.a. "Brooklyn Heavy." Boyd raced it with limited success on the East Coast. Photographer Ray Mann captured Leal's Camaro at Scottsdale, Arizona, in 1970. The photo was contributed by Quartermilestones.com.

California neighbors Butch Leal and Shirley Shahan towed all the way to Indy in 1971 to face each other on the quarter-mile. Leal's Mopar met Shahan's AMC in the first round of Eliminator. Shahan's Hornet was no match for her good friend Butch Leal and his mighty Mopar.

Longtime Mopar Pro Stock racer Butch Leal made the switch to Gil Kirk's The Rod Shop Pro Stock car in the 1980s. It was a great pairing of drag racing veterans, and the Kirk & Leal Pontiac did very well.

68   The Dawn of Pro Stock

didn't enjoy explosions or fires. He had seen a lot of his fellow Funny Car racers go through the blower learning curve and he wasn't interested in experiencing it himself. So Butch walked away from Funny Car racing and his car was purchased by Midwest funny car honcho Don Schumacher to become Schumacher's first *Stardust 'Cuda* funny car.

Leal seemed to disappear for almost three years. While most of drag racing didn't know what had happened to "The California Flash," his close friends knew that Butch had started golfing professionally.

One day toward the end of 1969, there was "The California Flash," returning to drag racing in Pro Stock. His debut in the class was a bit sour. He had teamed up with Mickey Thompson to field a Mustang powered by a 429-ci Shotgun Ford Hemi. The Mustang ran okay, but not up to Butch's and Mickey's expectations. So the project was scrapped and Leal was out of a ride early in the 1970 season. He quickly joined the Chevy Rebellion for 1970 in a new rat-motored Camaro now called the *Flashmobile*. Butch and his *California Flash* did fine, but a multitude of breakage problems plagued the Camaro throughout the season.

Tired of the parts breakage, Leal met with his old friends at Mopar. Could a Pixley farm boy join the Mopar factory racers for 1971? Plymouth welcomed Butch back into the Chrysler fold, so again the *California Flash* colors adorned a Plymouth factory race car. The next two years passed quickly for "Butch," as he shattered track records and beat the best of the best in Pro Stock around the country. "The California Flash" was back in a big way with readers of *Drag News*, who voted him Pro Stock Driver of the Year for the 1972 season.

Butch Leal was inactive in drag racing for the first half of the 1973 season; however, he came on strong in the second half, winning the NHRA Grand Nationals and the AHRA World Finals as well as numerous other track records. Leal ended the 1973 season with another *Drag News* Driver of the Year award. Team "Flash" debuted in 1974 and Leal added another car to his two-car field, a Pro Stock and a Plymouth Super Stock driven by old friend Gale Mortimer. Butch went on to have a few more good years with Mopar, but when Chrysler cut back its factory racers, Butch went golfing more often. A few more Mopar deals came Leal's way, but nothing like those of the mid 1960s and early 1970s.

This was one of the last of a long line of Mopar race cars raced by Butch Leal. The Pro Stock didn't set the world on fire either. So, do you know how Butch got his nickname, "The California Flash?" Leal was on tour in 1964 and promoter Ben Christ told Butch he needed a nickname to go with his driving style. Christ suggested "The California Flash," Butch loved it, and the rest is history!

Chapter Three

Photographer Mike Bagnod caught Butch Leal saying "bye-bye" to Lee Hunter's Ford Pinto at Fremont, California, in 1973. Butch was relatively inactive for the first half of the year, but came on strong in the last six months to score numerous track records at both AHRA and NHRA events. Wins at the NRHA Grand Nationals and the AHRA World Finals rounded out the year.

Both Leal and Sox came up through the ranks in drag racing and both had the chance to go big-time Funny Car racing, but the new Pro Stock Eliminator called to them and they settled into drag racing's newest Pro class. Sox and Leal were considered two of the best ever to pilot a Pro Stocker.

No stranger to a winner's circle, Butch Leal enjoyed his victory at the AHRA Winternationals at Scottsdale, Arizona, with Hurst's legendary Golden Shifter Girl, Linda Vaughn. Yet another win for "The California Flash!"

70   The Dawn of Pro Stock

The early 1980s saw Butch become a Pontiac driver, driving for the Gil Kirk Nationwise gang. Then, starting in 1984 Butch began a string of "bridesmaids," or runners-up at NHRA National events. In 1984, he was runner-up at the NHRA Cajun Nationals and the NHRA Winston Finals. The 1985 season saw three more NHRA National runner-up finishes in Pro Stock at Mile-High, the Summernationals, and the Grand Nationals. Finally, Leal took the Nationwise Pontiac to the winner's circle at the NHRA 1985 Southern Nationals. He won the Grand Nationals in 1986, as well as the NHRA Spring Nationals, but he returned to the runner-up position at several NHRA events in the late 1980s. Finally, he decided to call it a day and, you guessed it, return to the golf course and finally put drag racing behind him.

Wally Booth

In 1963, a likable Detroit resident by the name of Wally Booth was selling insurance to make a living. By 1965, he was piloting a 1962 Chevy 409 down the Michigan quarter-mile. Gathering all his automotive knowledge from automotive periodicals and various texts, Wally studied and blended what he had gathered from his own theories and put them to use in his next two race cars, a 1966 Chevelle followed by a 1967 model. The

Butch "The California Flash" Leal was voted Pro Stock driver of the year in 1972 and 1973 by the readers of Doris Herbert's Drag News. Drag News was considered by many to be a drag racers "bible." The weekly newspaper was filled with photos and stories from NHRA, AHRA, IHRA, and independent dragstrips in North America. The "bible" was sold at racetracks and hundreds of speed shops across the country and Canada.

When Butch Leal and I got together for a photo shoot, anything could happen—and often did. Yes, that is Butch doing a fire burnout at Orange County International Raceway (OCIR) for the cover of Drag Racing USA magazine. Butch and I had never seen a Pro Stocker do a fire burnout, so we figured, "What the heck, let's light Butch's new Butler-built Pro Stock on fire!" We got our cover shot, but OCIR's manager Mike Jones wasn't happy about our attempt at burning a hole in the bleach box area.

Chapter Three

1967 was an SS/D and won its class at the Winternationals, Spring Nationals, and U.S. Nationals.

Then, as 1968 dawned, Booth acquired a Camaro with a 375-hp, 396-ci engine. The Camaro battled all year with Ford's new 428-ci Cobra Jet Mustangs to no avail, as he couldn't pull out a class win in 1968. His brightest moment was being runner-up to Arlen Vanke in Super Stock Eliminator at the Nationals.

Booth opened 1969 by driving a Mopar, which lasted about six months, then went back to the Camaro and started match race competition in Pro Stock. The Motown racer's "book learning" approach to drag racing produced one of the most unorthodox combinations ever seen at any early Pro Stock event. Booth stuck with his 427 Chevy engine, but got rid of the Chevy drivetrain and replaced it with Chrysler components, including the transmission, drivetrain, and rear end. So much for an "all-Chevy" Camaro!

In mid 1970, Booth became a Detroit "Rat Pack" Pro Stocker, with Dick Arons building the engines for Wally's Pro Stock ride. The team of Booth and Arons did well on the match race circuit and, when time

Wally Booth (of Michigan) and Royce Freeman (of Texas) were two of the early privateers in the Pro Stock class, and they faced off at Dallas, Texas, in 1970. Booth spent many hours reading any manual and other information on engines, transmissions, etc. You might say the Michigan-based racer competed by the book. Freeman only raced in the Pro Stock class for a few years and then dropped back into the Super Stock ranks.

When American Motors decided to go Pro Stock racing seriously, Wally Booth was the one to receive the call. His Gremlin X was the other half of team American Motors Pro Stock Racing. Dick Maskin and Jim Gilbert raced the other half of the team.

The Competitors

permitted, they also raced NHRA national events. Wally received a big break in the early 1970s when American Motors decided to enter the Pro Stock wars, NHRA-style. He and his *Gremlin X* represented American Motors in the ongoing Pro Stock wars. Booth teamed with the Maskin & Kannors Hornet, giving American Motors a two-car Pro Stock team.

The saga of Wally Booth came to an abrupt end when American Motors suddenly departed from motorsports. A very disappointed Booth returned to his business with Dick Arons and raced a Chevy Vega Pro Stocker for a short while.

Herb "Mr. 4 Speed" McCandless

So, can you tell me who won the first NHRA U.S. Nationals Pro Stock Eliminator? If you said Herb McCandless, you would be correct. That boy from Memphis, Tennessee, took home the big prize at the 1970 NHRA U.S. Nationals driving the Sox & Martin number-two team car. When rare problems (broken transmission) sidelined the number-one Sox & Martin Pro Stock entry in the second round at the U.S. Nationals, Herb was there to claim top prize in Pro Stock against fellow Mopar racer "Akron" Arlen Vanke.

At the NHRA U.S. Nationals in 1970, Herb McCandless took the Sox & Martin number-two team car to the first NHRA U.S. Nationals Pro Stock honors. McCandless carried the Sox & Martin colors to victory when Ronnie Sox (in the number-one team car) broke a transmission, leaving the number-two car to battle for the Pro Stock Eliminator title. Here, independent racer Melvin Yow fell to "Mr. 4 Speed" McCandless.

With the failure of the American Motors Pro Stock venture, Wally Booth returned to his Chevy roots and went racing with a Dick Arons–powered Vega, which ran very well on the match race circuit and at a few chosen national events. There would be no more selling insurance for Booth!

The Dawn of Pro Stock

Chapter Three

The 1972 National Challenge at Tulsa, Oklahoma, produced one heck of a controversial race in Pro Stock. John Hagen lined up against Herb McCandless in the semi-final and the winner was to race Bill Jenkins for $25,000 in prize money, the largest purse ever for Pro Stock. Both cars did burnouts, and starter Pete Talmadge signaled them to the starting line. Hagen staged his Mopar while McCandless' Sox & Martin crew took their time adjusting McCandless' wheelie bars. Starter Talmadge counted down the seconds allowed for McCandless to stage his Mopar. Hagen was told to make a single run for the win, disqualifying McCandless. A violent argument ensued, but starter Talmadge stood firm on his decision. The Sox & Martin crew went crying to the AHRA and track officials to reverse Talmadge's decision. They ended up reversing the decision, and thus there was a re-run between Hagen and McCandless. McCandless won the re-run against Hagen. Did Hagen get the short end? What do you think?

Herb McCandless heads for the moon with his Sox & Martin–prepared Pro Stock Mopar. McCandless tested the bite at NHRA's Summernationals at Englishtown, New Jersey. Herb hurt the front end when landing after this wheelstand and lost the race. Wheelie bars, anyone?

74   The Dawn of Pro Stock

The Competitors

At Scottsdale, Arizona, in 1970, Herb McCandless had a small blip in his driving career when he experienced handling problems with his Super Stock Dodge. McCandless' wild ride resulted in a crunched car and wall, but no one was hurt in this embarrassing crash.

Chapter Three

One of the best moves Sox & Martin made was choosing a driver for their number-two Pro Stock car. They hired the talented Super Stock driver Herb McCandless in 1970 and he did very well for Sox & Martin, and also for "Brooklyn Heavy" and his own Sox & Martin-prepped Pro Stocker. This photo was contributed by Ray Mann/Quartermilestones.com.

Let's go back to McCandless' humble beginnings in drag racing, sometime in 1962, when Herb sat behind the wheel of his 1962 409 Chevrolet, his "training wheels" in drag racing. Then, in 1964, he was racing a B/MPO Chevy and the next year Herb acquired one of the Plymouth Super Stockers. His Super Stock car was one of ten built with a four-speed manual transmission. Herb's version was the only one racing in the South, so his reputation as a smooth shifter spread among his fellow racers, earning him the nickname "Mr. 4 Speed."

When Super Stock rules were changed to permit any tire size, Herb's 1968 Hemi-Dart became one of the fastest rides in the country. After earning a ride behind the wheel in Billy "The Kid" Stepp's 'Cuda, Herb collected modified eliminator honors at the first NHRA Gatornationals in 1970. Meanwhile, Sox & Martin were on the lookout for a talented young driver for their number-two team Pro Stock car, and Herb was given the opportunity to shine in drag racing's newest Eliminator class.

In May 1970, Herb was hired full-time by Sox & Martin, which was a great move for the bespectacled young man from Memphis. Not only did Herb drive for Sox & Martin, but he worked side-by-side with Jake King, Dave Christie, and Joe Fisher, the team's brain trust at the race shop in Burlington, North Carolina. The quiet guy from Memphis put the Sox & Martin Mopar in many a winner's circle and match raced at numerous national events. Herb went on to race his own Sox & Martin–prepped Pro Stocker and made his mark in early Pro Stock class racing.

Melvin Yow

In Lillington, North Carolina, in 1956, there was a young Melvin Yow co-driving his car club's Ford Gasser. Yow was one of the many youthful drivers learning to drag race at the area's local dragstrip. He soon caught the "need for speed" and set his sights on the Super Stock classes. His first foray into the Super Stock arena found him behind the wheel of a 413-powered Plymouth, and shortly after that a 426 Wedge took the place of the 413.

In 1965, fate smiled on Yow by pairing him with local businessman T. W. Grissom, and together the duo fielded the fastest legal A/FX race cars in the country. While most of the Mopar A/FX owners were switching

Independent racer Melvin Yow parked his Mopar Pro Stocker and joined the Billy Stepp team effort in 1973. Yow did well for Stepp on the Pro Stock match race circuit, and then, in 1974, Yow only drove in the first few major events before vacating the Stepp-owned Duster. This photo was taken by John Shanks in 1973 at the NHRA Winternationals.

The Competitors

Melvin Yow faced off with Don Carlton at the NHRA Spring Nationals at Columbus, Ohio. The Mopar Missile *prevailed, and also took home the best engineered award at the event. Yes, the* Mopar Missile *was just the* Motown Missile *with a name change. Legend has it that the Motown records people were not happy about a race car with the word "Motown" on its doors. Henceforth, the* Mopar Missile *was born, and the Motown Records folks were happy.*

to altered wheelbases and 2,600 pounds, Yow & Grissom stayed true to the legal class rules. In 1966, Yow & Grissom set B/FX and C/FX NHRA national records. At the end of the 1966 season, Melvin ventured out on his own. Racing out of his Lillington, North Carolina, auto repair shop, he split his time between work and racing his 1967 SS/B Dodge, and then in 1968 he opened behind the wheel of an SS/B Hemi Dart.

When NHRA's new Pro Stock class began in 1970, Melvin quickly converted his SS/B Hemi Dart to Pro Stock trim and got ready for the Pro Stock class. That entire year was a learning curve for him, and with that knowledge applied to his new 1971 Challenger in Pro Stock, he was ready for the 1971 season. The 1971 season proved to be frustrating, but a definite learning experience for Yow. His Challenger ran nose to nose with the factory "big boys" and reached the semi-finals and final rounds at quite a few national events. Melvin even clocked the quickest time for a legal NHRA Pro Stock car at an amazing 9.25 seconds, and in a match race the Yow Challenger broke into the 8.90-second range.

When Billy "The Kid" Stepp decided to race a two-car team, he made an offer to Yow he couldn't refuse, making him a part of the mighty Stepp Pro Stock race team. Melvin did very well for Stepp on the match race and national event circuit. Then, in 1974, after a few events, the team was no more and Yow dropped off the face of the drag racing earth. Stepp continued racing, but Yow was nowhere to be found. While writing this book, I contacted three of the best historians of the sport of drag racing, Bret Kepner, John Jodauga, and Bob Frey, but none of them could pinpoint what had happened to him. So I am assuming that Yow simply returned to his family and business in Lillington, North Carolina, and moved on with his life.

Hubert "The Mouth of the South" Platt

I guess you could say Hubert Platt made a full circle, from Super Stock to A/FX Funny Cars and back to Pro Stock. Platt first came to fame as one of those "Southern Style" match racers such as Don Nicholson, Ronnie Sox, and Phil Bonner. This group all had a hand in laying

Here in 1966 at Fremont, California, Hubert Platt piloted a long-nosed A/FX Ford Mustang down the quarter-mile. In the other lane was Chevy rival, the late Dickie Harrell. Platt raced hard in the A/FX class throughout the United States.

The Dawn of Pro Stock

Chapter Three

Hubert "The Mouth of the South" Platt was a true showman for the Pro Stock class, and the fans loved his funny-car-style burnouts. Since Platt had driven in the early Funny Car class, he had lots of practice in the art of the burnout.

After Ford dropped Platt, Hubert was back to being a privateer. While his Maverick did okay, it didn't pose any threat to the heavy hitters at national events. Match racing was Platt's bread and butter and the fans loved his big-time burnouts and wheels-up runs.

The Competitors

Hubert Platt (left) and his crew celebrate a victory in Pro Stock Eliminator at the 1971 Las Vegas Open. This was a rare national win for Platt, who limited his racing mainly to match racing and a few national events required by his Ford factory sponsorship deal.

Hubert Platt at the Super Stock Reunion in Virginia in 1996.

Hubert Platt was just starting to get his Ford Pinto dialed in when Ford pulled the rug out from underneath him. Major cutbacks in Ford's racing program left Platt out in the cold. Platt shook off his misfortune and stayed in racing as a privateer on the Pro Stock match racing circuit. Not much can stop "The Mouth of the South" from drag racing!

The Dawn of Pro Stock

Chapter Three

the groundwork for the popularity of stock-bodied drag machines. Partnering with Nicholson in 1963, Platt and Nicholson ruled the match race circuit in 1963 Chevrolets. Then, in 1964 Nicholson switched to Mercury, and Platt found himself at the controls of a factory-backed Ford Thunderbolt Super Stocker. Not satisfied with his very fast Thunderbolt, he soon took the wheel of a 10-second factory Ford Falcon.

Platt match raced his Falcon around the Southeastern United States during 1965 and around mid-season replaced his ride with a new, long-nosed altered-wheelbase Mustang. The Mustang proved to be a huge success for Platt. His wild wheelstands and match race wins made him a fan favorite, and promoters wanted the "Hue Baby" at their racetracks. Just when things were looking really bright for this Georgia drag racer, fate stepped in and his Mustang was totaled in a towing accident. However, around that time a ride opened up in one of the best-running A/XS-injected Mustangs in the country. So into Dick Brannan's Mustang went Hubert Platt, along with a sponsorship by Paul Harvey Ford. That Mustang, with Platt at the wheel, became one of the best running Fords, with 8.50-second ETs, second only to the Mercury Comets.

As 1967 came around, Platt switched his ride again, this time into a factory 427 Ford Fairlane in the SS/B class. His solid 10-second Fairlane was then replaced with a new Cobra Jet Mustang in 1968. Then, in 1969, Ford had something special in store for Platt. He was selected, along with fellow Georgia racer Randy Payne, to head up Ford's Super Car Clinic program. The two Southern gentlemen drag racers proved to be a big hit with Ford dealers as well as the attending Ford fans. Just when things were looking good for "Hue Baby," the ceiling fell in. Ford pulled the plug on their racing program, did away with the clinics, and cut all racing support. Hubert Platt was now a privateer with no sponsor.

Being a racer with the gift of gab, he hit the bricks, knocking on doors and managing to get help from Delta Airlines and Falstaff Beer, both new sponsors in the world of Pro Stock racing. Even without factory sponsorship, Hubert held his own against the factory-backed Pro Stockers. Paul Harvey Ford was once again on the side of Hubert's Mustang and Maverick Pro Stock cars. Then, in 1973, Platt ran a Ford Pinto in Pro Stock and did very well with help from his sponsors. But, without factory backing and big sponsor dollars, "Hue Baby" faded from the Pro Stock wars. Hubert Platt was certainly one Southern gentleman who left his mark on early Pro Stock racing. Long live "The Mouth of the South!"

Barrie Poole

No one could argue that the 1970 and 1971 Pro Stock seasons were dominated by Ronnie Sox and Chrysler, and in 1972, Bill Jenkins ruled the NHRA Pro Stock class with his Vega. However, as 1973 dawned, hope was in the air for the Ford Motor Company faithful at NHRA national events. Since the birth of the Pro Stock class, Don Nicholson had been carrying the Ford effort, but a new Ford Pro Stock star was emerging from obscurity: Barrie Poole. He had already become the first Canadian to win a major NHRA national title when he took top Super Stock honors at the 1970 Winternationals. With partner John Elliot, the duo also won the Spring Nationals and scored a runner-up at the Summernationals.

The NHRA Winternationals brought them another win in 1971 and then victory at a *Popular Hot Rodding* meet, and the team began venturing into Pro Stock with a 427-ci Wedge-powered Comet. Their new entry into Pro Stock did not fare well or impress anyone. Right after the NHRA U.S. Nationals in 1972, the team finished its newest entry in Pro Stock, a shiny new Pinto. Right

Canadian Barrie Poole started his Pro Stock career by lining up with crafty Pro Stock veteran Butch Leal at the AHRA Winternationals in Scottsdale, Arizona, in 1972. Leal gave Poole a lesson in Pro Stock driving and defeated this new Poole/Elliott Comet Pro Stock.

out of the box, it ran a 9.65-second ET at 7.01 pounds per square inch.

Just when it seemed Ford had another star in Pro Stock, Poole went snowmobiling in his native home Canada and had a very serious crash. Just like that, Poole's Pro Stock career ended. He recovered from his serious injuries, but never drove a race car again. The new Pro Stock Pinto was sold to the Gapp & Roush team, and we all know what took place after they got their hands on it.

Wayne Gapp

Another early hero in Pro Stock was Wayne Gapp, and his march toward Pro Stock greatness began in 1966 with the purchase of George DeLorean's 1965 A/FX Mercury Comet. Gapp proved his worth as a driver when he quickly set the new B/XS national record with his new ride. When the Comet proved to be too slow for Wayne, he began racing a gas-burning Cougar funny car in 1967. The Cougar clocked in the low 9-second range at 150 mph with its SOHC 427-ci engine under the hood.

Then, in 1969, it was out with the Cougar body and in with a Mustang shell. Gone was the SOHC 427 and in its place was a Boss 429. With those changes, Gapp became the head engineer at Ford for the development of the Boss 429 in 1970, and this played a major role in the engine's success at NASCAR races.

The Pro Stock final at the 1973 NHRA Gatornationals was an all-Ford-Pinto finale. "Dyno" Don Nicholson put away Wayne Gapp, who was driving the Gapp & Roush entry. Nicholson ran a 9.4 to vanquish a losing 9.3 for "sleepy" Wayne Gapp.

Ford and Chevy clashed at the 1975 NHRA U.S. Nationals. Wayne Gapp drove the Gapp & Roush Ford and put New York's Richie Zul and his Camaro back on the trailer for the 1975 NHRA U.S. Nationals Pro Stock title. John Shanks was there to capture the action.

Chapter Three

The team of Gapp & Roush has long been associated with Dearborn products even before they joined forces in 1971. Once the duo gelled, it was "look out, world of Pro Stock." Gapp & Roush became a force to reckon with from 1971 to 1975.

In 1971, Gapp & Roush joined forces and campaigned a Boss 429-powered four-door Ford Maverick. Earlier in 1970, Gapp had become the head engineer at Ford, and he played a major role in the engine's success in NASCAR racing. In 1971, the pair was handed the task of developing the Boss 429 powerplant for Ford Motor Company as it applied to drag racing.

Like many Pro Stock racers in the mid-to-late 1970s, Gapp & Roush were very, very busy during the racing season. To satisfy all the promoters, they put a second and sometimes third car on the Pro Stock circuit. One of the team drivers for Gapp & Roush's Ford was Ken Dondero, who was a journeyman driver for Nicholson, Jenkins, and Gapp & Roush, which is not a bad resume for a former A/G and BB/GS driver from Northern California. Photographer Mike Bagnod captured this action at Pomona, California, in 1974.

82 The Dawn of Pro Stock

The Competitors

In 1972, Gapp & Roush did fairly well with their Ford Pinto in Pro Stock, but with the arrival of small-block power (thanks to Jenkins' 1972 Vega), they and Bob Glidden built a new Pinto for 1973, incorporating all the best new changes for the NHRA Pro Stock class.

It was Ford versus Mopar at Scottsdale, Arizona, in 1973. The Michigan-based Pro Stock Gapp & Roush debuted a new, budget, small-block Ford Pinto Pro Stock at the 1973 AHRA Winternationals against Ohio's Billy Stepp, with Melvin Yow at the controls.

The Dawn of Pro Stock

Chapter Three

With the constant weight and other rule changes, 1974 saw the debut of the Gapp & Roush Mustang II–based Pro Stock car. Here at the 1974 NHRA Gatornationals, Gapp & Roush race East Coast–based Paul Blevins' Chevy Vega.

Gapp & Roush introduced their Tijuana Taxi in 1975, which was a four-door Ford Maverick with the rear doors welded shut. They moved to a Maverick to avoid the weight handicaps that were put on Pintos. And because the Maverick had a longer wheelbase, it wasn't weight handicapped by the NHRA. The 1975 racing season proved to be the last year of Pro Stock for Gapp & Roush, as Jack Roush went NASCAR racing after the season ended and Wayne Gapp continued to work for Ford.

Making the cover of Drag News was like being on the cover of Time magazine for any drag racer. Here Gapp & Roush's Ford Pinto Pro Stock is featured on the October 20, 1973, cover. The Michigan duo had won the NHRA World Finals and set a new national record in Pro Stock.

84   The Dawn of Pro Stock

The Competitors

Everything changed when Ford decided that Gapp's involvement in their racing program as a principal engineer and his racing business were in conflict, and they gave him an ultimatum: Give up one or the other. At that point, a friend introduced Wayne to someone who could run the business while Wayne stayed on at Ford. It turned out to be Jack Roush, a former Ford employee.

The partnership of Wayne Gapp and Jack Roush commenced in 1971 when the duo campaigned a Maverick with (of course) a Boss 429 Ford power plant. It took most of the NHRA season to work the bugs out of the Maverick, so you would think it would do well in 1972, right? Not so fast, as that guy named Jenkins showed what small-block power could do in a Pro Stock Vega, and it was back to the drawing board for the Ford guys from Michigan.

A new Pinto soon had the Gapp & Roush logo on its doors. This car ran okay, but it never wowed Ford or Ford fans. It was subsequently sold to some Indiana racer named Glidden, and a new small-block-powered Pinto was on the drawing board. Even though they had sold the Pinto to Glidden, they continued helping him and also Barrie Poole with the technical aspects of racing the Pinto, gaining some very useful knowledge that they then applied to their new 1973 Pinto. That car ran very well, and soon promoters from all across the United States wanted the Gapp & Roush Pinto for Pro Stock match races, etc. This was great, but match racing and national events are two entirely different styles of racing.

NHRA events had very strict rules on weight, engine displacement, and numerous other factors. To resolve this problem, the team introduced a second car for WCS and national events. Their friend and customer Barrie Poole had suffered a terrible driving career-ending snowmobile accident, so Gapp & Roush purchased the Poole & Elliot Pinto for match racing, and now it was a two-car Pro Stock operation. During the next five years, Gapp & Roush raced one of the premier Ford Pro Stockers in drag racing, and when Jack Roush got the itch to go NASCAR racing in 1976, the team quietly folded... much to the chagrin of their fans in drag racing.

Dave Strickler

Dave Strickler seems to be a forgotten name in early Pro Stock racing. When this York, Pennsylvania, native partnered with Bill Jenkins in the early 1960s, the records began to fall. Strickler banged the four-speed manual transmission in the Jenkins-tuned Chevys and the Pennsylvania duo's exploits reached from coast to coast in Super Stock racing. When Strickler and Jenkins split, Strickler went A/FX racing and Jenkins stayed in Super Stock, driving and tuning his own cars. At the 1963 NHRA Nationals, Dave won the A/FX class and also took home the little eliminator trophy at the same event. After that, he flirted with a Mopar A/FXer for the next couple years before debuting an A/XS long-nosed Corvette in 1966.

The new NHRA A/XS class boasted drivers such as Ronnie Sox and the Ramchargers, so Dave joined them with a new A/XS Corvette he built from the ground up. Not only could he drive, but he also built the tube chassis and 427-inch nitro-burning Chevy engine. In fact, the more horsepower Dave made with his 427 Chevy, the more ill-handling the 'Vette became. After racing for part of the year in 1967 and finding no improvement in handling, Dave took the 'Vette back to the shop in

This was Dave Strickler's evil self-built Corvette Factory Experimental that he raced for the entire 1967 season. However, when he finally returned home to Pennsylvania at the end of the racing season, he stripped the 'Vette, pushed it into an alley adjoining his shop, and burned it to the ground. Strickler destroyed the 'Vette instead of selling it because he didn't want anyone killed or injured in a car he had built.

Chapter Three

Not many Pro Stocks came out of the Sunshine State; however, Bo Law's Camaro was a nice representative for Florida. In the far lane is Pennsylvania's Dave Strickler and his Old Reliable Camaro. The veteran racer took this round from the Florida-based Camaro.

Dave Strickler drove for Bill Jenkins, but really made his own mark in drag racing with his Old Reliable IV Chevy. With a sponsorship from his father-in-law, Strickler terrorized the stock classes with his Impala.

Dave Strickler drove for friend Bill Jenkins, and he successfully raced his own line of Old Reliable stock (and Pro Stock) class cars. Strickler passed away suddenly at the young age of forty-four, which was a great loss to his friends, family, and the racing community as a whole.

86   The Dawn of Pro Stock

The Competitors

The one track Strickler seemed to excel at was his home strip of York US 30, where he was the unofficial king. Throughout his racing career, Strickler primarily match raced and occasionally competed in a few select national events. The last Pro Stock car Dave raced was a Chevy Vega, and then he retired in 1974 to devote time to his family and business.

Pennsylvania, stripped the car of the engine and racing components, put the car in the alley, and set it on fire to burn it to the ground. Dave didn't want anyone else driving the ill-handling 'Vette, not wanting anyone to die or get hurt in a car he had built.

After Strickler's adventure in the A/XS class, he returned to the stock classes. In 1970, he once again drove for his ol' buddy Bill Jenkins in the new Pro Stock Eliminator category. Although it was only a short stint behind the wheel of Jenkins Pro Stock Camaro, Strickler was hooked. Soon, the Strickler trademark name "Ol' Reliable" was being carried by a shiny new Chevy Pro Stock car.

Where Strickler's "Ol' Reliable" trademark name came from is an interesting story. Ammon R. Smith first opened his Chevrolet dealership just outside of York, Pennsylvania, in 1912 and the the local folks called his dealership "Ol' Reliable." Strickler's bride was Suzie Smith, daughter of Ammon R. Smith, which afforded him considerable backing by Chevrolet at Smith's dealership. So young Strickler held on to a great sponsorship from his father-in-law even after Ammon passed away in 1966.

Dave raced in Pro Stock for about four years, and since he had promised his wife (and himself) that if he couldn't make money racing professionally he would quit, so he did. He continued building engines for other stock and pro stock racers until 1985, when Dave passed away suddenly at the age of forty-four from heart disease. It was a huge loss for the fans, family, and friends of this pioneer drag racer.

Don Carlton

The one thing I have learned about drag racers is that they come from all walks of life and a wide selection of professions. Don Carlton was a prime example of this as he came out of the furniture factories of Lenoir, North Carolina, to become one of the best of the best Pro Stock drivers in those early days of the class. He labored at his factory job for eight hours, returned home to work on his "weekend warrior" drag car, and raced that weekend. His talent behind the wheel earned him winnings that he turned around and put back into the

Chapter Three

At the beginning of 1971, a mild-mannered, bespectacled Don Carlton took over the driving chores of the high-tech Motown Missile Pro Stock. The former furniture worker from North Carolina made the most of his first big-time Pro Stock ride. Carlton proved to be one of the most talented Pro Stock drivers to venture down the quarter-mile.

In this image provided by Quartermilestones.com, Don Carlton launches the Motown Missile at Martin, Michigan, in 1971. In the upper left of this photo is a photographer in a light jacket and dark pants. That is yours truly, shooting coverage for Popular Hot Rodding. I rarely saw photos of myself working back in the good ol' days. This race proved to be the Motown Missile's first major Pro Stock Eliminator title. The track was home to the largest independent major drag race, the Popular Hot Rodding Championships.

It's the Mopar Missile, a.k.a. the former Motown Missile. The reason for the name change was that Berry Gordy's Motown Records didn't want anyone confusing the car with his record company in Detroit. Different name, same group of brainiacs: Tom Coddington, Ted Spehar, Joe Pappas, Dick Oldfield, Al Adam, Clyde Hodges, Ron Killen, and of course, Don Carlton.

88   The Dawn of Pro Stock

The Competitors

The second major AHRA race in 1971 was the Florida Grand American at West Palm Beach, Florida. Don Carlton and the highly engineered Motown Missile collected their first major victory for the year. Carlton defeated upstart independent Jim Hayter in the final round. Note the slick plastic shields on the front wheels to improve airflow.

car, a vicious circle most drag racers endured throughout the 1960s. By 1970, Carlton was racing against full-time racing teams, which was something a weekend racer couldn't keep up with on the quarter-mile or within his budget.

Chrysler racing honchos could really spot talent, so they reached out to pluck Don Carlton out of the furniture factory and made him a factory racer. Chrysler's ultra-high-tech *Motown Missile* race team now had a new member. Carlton joined Ted Speher (engine builder), Lenny Bartush (Ted's assistant), John Baumann (carb wizard), Tom Coddington, Al Adam, and Ron Killen to form the *Motown Missile* Pro Stock team. Carlton became the driver of the Ron Butler/Dick Oldfield–built Mopar Pro Stock car. Between 1970 and 1977, Pro Stock fans and racers got to know Don Carlton and the *Motown Missile*, and later the *Mopar Missile*, very well. Carlton's battles with Jenkins, Sox, and Nicholson are legendary in the sport of drag racing.

All of that came to a horrific end on July 5, 1977, at Milan, Michigan, when Carlton crashed and rolled while testing his Colt Pro Stock. He died of head injuries at only thirty-six years old and the mild-mannered, talented, Pro Stock driver was gone.

Chapter Three

The 1972 NHRA Gatornationals marked a milestone for Don Carlton when he notched his first major NHRA Pro Stock Eliminator victory with ETs of 9.58, 9.56, 9.55, and 9.55. His opponent was privateer Melvin Yow, who red-lighted in the final round.

At the 1973 NHRA Winternationals in Pomona, California, fans were delighted to find a Don versus Don match-up in the Pro Stock final. "Dyno" Don Nicholson's Ford Pinto edged out Don Carlton's *Mopar Missile* with a fantastic 9.33 in the final round. Carlton had qualified first with a 9.22, and Nicholson wrapped up second with a 9.38.

In 1974, the *Mopar Missile* was transferred by Chrysler to Don Carlton, and then Stewart Pomeroy purchased it from Carlton, putting Kenny Hahn in the driver's seat. Carlton went racing with his Dodge Colt under **The Rod Shop** banner, not in Pro Stock but in Comp Eliminator. This photo was obtained from John Shanks.

The Competitors

Before his untimely death in 1977, Don Carlton had won six major NHRA events and one major win in five consecutive years. Not too bad for a North Carolina furniture worker.

On July 5, 1977, at Milan Drag Way in Milan, Michigan, Don Carlton lost his life at the age of thirty-six in his 1976 Dodge Colt. They never were able to find any mechanical problems on the wrecked race car, which they later buried in a landfill.

Other Movers and Shakers

One of the early tough guy privateers of the Pro Stock drivers, Jim Hayter, left the Stock and Super Stock ranks because he was tired of handicap drag racing. Jim was an independent guy who matched his 1969 Camaro Pro Stocker against some of the finest racers in 1970, and he did quite well. His friend Chuck Wright helped with some money, and Hayter had Diamond Racing engines as a co-sponsor of the car. With no backing from large sponsors, Jim had to do pretty much everything himself. He did the chassis work, tuned the big 427-inch Diamond-prepared Chevy engine, drove the car, etc. Believe it or not, even without the sponsor money, Hayter managed to give the factory cars a run for the Pro Stock gold in NHRA and AHRA.

Another racer deserving mention is Arlen Vanke, whom I classify as one of those early unsung heroes of the Pro Stock class. Known as "Akron" Arlen to his pals, this Akron, Ohio-based racer was a strong contender in any class he raced, whether it was Super Stock or Pro Stock. Driving his trademark black-and-yellow Mopar, Arlen primarily tested prototype parts for Chrysler engineering. In the first year of the NHRA Pro Stock class, Arlen was runner-up to Ronnie Sox four times at national events. He finally broke out of his "bridesmaid" role by winning the 1971 AHRA Winternationals Pro Stock eliminator.

The 1960s funny car star, Dick Loehr, sold his Stampede *blown Ford Mustang funny car to Texan Bob Veleska and became a Ford drag racing team member. Afterward, Loehr took delivery of a shining Pro Stock Maverick courtesy of the Ford Motor company.*

The Dawn of Pro Stock

Chapter Three

Having covered the early hero drivers of the Pro Stock class and just about all the mainstay racers that were driver/owners of their race teams, what about the racers who were the money men/owners? These individuals watched and rooted from the sidelines as "rent-a-drivers" piloted their four-wheeled investments down the quarter-mile. The two most famous (or should I say infamous) of the early era of Pro Stock owners were Billy "The Kid" Stepp and Rufus "Brooklyn Heavy" Boyd.

William Elias Stepp was the son of an Appalachian lay minister, a tough, strong kid, a brawler, and also a very smart person. Stepp was one of the most gracious and polite people I dealt with in the world of Pro Stock racing. It was true that Stepp was a gangster. He "owned" the city of Dayton, Ohio, and controlled all the rackets in the city. I photographed one of his first Pro Stock Mopars, and Billy loved the attention drag racing brought him. After the article appeared with the photos that I had taken, Stepp took care of me any time I passed through Dayton. Women, alcohol, and motel rooms were no problem. If I wanted a nice dinner at the best restaurants in Dayton, I just mentioned Stepp's name and the tab was taken care of by the restaurant.

Stepp loved drag racing, especially the Pro Stock class, and his list of "rent-a-drivers" read like a who's who of extraordinary drag racing drivers. It included Don Carlton, Melvin Yow, Stu McDade, Ronnie Sox, and Bobby Yowell.

Billy was certainly a colorful guy. He did a photo shoot with my old friend Don Green of *Hot Rod* magazine that was absolutely classic. Stepp and his crew wore 1930s-style gangster attire, and Stepp held a Thompson submachine gun with a "moll" draped on his right shoulder. The gang stood around the car, which was sitting in a Dayton cemetery. This photo shoot from 1973 is still a classic to many Pro Stock fans, and Billy "The Kid" Stepp has to be one of the most flamboyant Pro Stock owners to compete during those early years.

There was an East Coast version of Stepp as well, Rufus "Brooklyn Heavy" Boyd. "Heavy" was a big-time street racer located in none other than Brooklyn, New York. He was a large, black man who loved drag racing and street racing. His business was called Heavy Racing Enterprises, which included quite a stable of drag cars, including Bill Jenkins' 1970 Camaro that had won Pro Stock at the NHRA Winternationals and NHRA Gatornationals, as well as Butch Leal's 1970 Camaro Pro Stocker.

Stories abound about "Heavy's" exploits as a New York City street racer, with thousands of dollars exchanging hands on a single run, including one winner-take-all purse of $250,000 on just one race. Other tales were told

Quartermilestones.com provided this shot of one of the lesser known privateers of Pro Stock, Mike Fons, toiling on his Pro Stock Camaro somewhere on the East Coast. A few years later, Fons was a very respected driver/owner in Pro Stock Eliminator.

The Competitors

In those early days of Pro Stock, the Motown Missile *gang were the high-tech gurus of the Pro Stock class. The* Missile *was state of the art in Pro Stock for 1970. The Chrysler brain trust included the team of Dick Maxwell, Ted Spehar, Mike Koran, Tom Hoover, Leonard Bartush, Dick Oldfield, Tom Coddington, Al Adam, and John Bauman. The product they produced was considered the world's finest engineered Pro Stock in drag racing. Photographer John Shanks captured this image of the* Motown Missile *at Ontario, California, in 1970.*

Photographer John Shanks caught some serious pit action by Billy Stepp and his crew at Pomona, California, in 1970. Yes, that is Stepp in the lower right corner working away on his race car. Who says Stepp wasn't a hands-on owner?

The 1971 season opened in Scottsdale, Arizona, at the AHRA Winternationals. Two of the finest in Pro Stock, Arlen Vanke (with his Ohio-based Mopar) and Pennsylvania's Bill "Grumpy" Jenkins (with his new 1971 Chevy Camaro) went head to head. "Akron" Arlen defeated Bob Lambeck in the final and claimed 1971s first Pro Stock major victory.

The Dawn of Pro Stock

Chapter Three

about "Heavy" showing up at a big Pro Stock race at an East Coast track with a suitcase full of cash and calmly purchasing the entire Sox & Martin race team, including the car, truck, tools, and spare engines, right in the pits!

Another favorite story is told about his race team's "invasion" of Capitol Race Way, Maryland, one evening. Apparently, "Heavy" and his posse of thirteen race cars showed up complete with trailers. He had a problem getting his cars through tech, but he was undaunted and approached Juilo Marro, the promoter at Capital Raceway, and the *Brooklyn Heavy Eliminator* was quickly established for the evening.

Alas, the federal government eventually caught up with "Heavy" in late 1972 with a raid on his home,

Billy "The Kid" Stepp not only raced a Pro Stock Mopar, but his team included a Super Stock 'Cuda that always seemed to be in the money rounds wherever it raced.

When Rufus "Brooklyn Heavy" Boyd had major legal issues, he was forced to sell his race cars, and there were a lot of them in his stables. Old friend and Pro Stock racer Carmen Rotunda stepped in and purchased part of Boyd's Pro Stock fleet, including a race car, truck, and tools.

In 1972, the wealthiest drag race took place at a small racetrack in Tulsa, Oklahoma, where a Professional Racers Association (PRA) race featured Top Fuel, Funny Car, and Pro Stock cars from all across the United States, with more than $25,000 in cash and goodies at stake for the winner of each Pro class. On his way to winning the jackpot for Pro Stock, Bill Jenkins defeated a very tough Butch Leal in the semi-finals. It was just two weeks prior to this race that Jenkins' Vega was stolen at an AHRA race in St. Louis, Missouri. It was recovered shortly thereafter, sans front clip, doors, and engine/transmission. Jenkins and crew worked frantically to get the Vega back in business for the race in Tulsa, and obviously it was worth the extra effort.

netting one-and-a-half million dollars in cash. "Heavy" was charged with money laundering and trafficking heroin, and was sentenced to twenty-five years in a federal prison. This memorable character, who so loved drag racing, was now out of action, but he did leave his mark on early Pro Stock racing. His drivers, including Ronnie Lyles, Herb McCandless, Carmen Rotunda, and others, went on to greater ventures in Pro Stock.

Mike Fons started out a lowly privateer with a Pro Stock Camaro and worked his way into some extraordinary rides in the early days of Pro Stock racing. Mike could really get the fans cheering with his wheels-up launches and smoke-filled burnouts, proving to be a fan favorite on the match race circuit.

With most of the Pro Stock racers coming from the Super Stock ranks, "Akron" Arlen Vanke was no exception. The Midwest-based Vanke did very well in the Super Stock class and proved to be one heck of a Pro Stock competitor during the infant years of the class.

Chapter Three

This smilin' guy is "Akron" Arlen Vanke in 2011. These days, Vanke can be found with his retro Pro Stock at many of the nostalgia drag races throughout the Midwest and along the East Coast. Arlen loves to meet his fans, and he can bench race with anyone from the early days of Pro Stock. Just ask him about 96 pounds, and then stand back for the answer.

Photographer Don Gillespie stumbled upon a Pro Stock photo shoot at the closed-forever Lions Drag Strip where Hot Rod magazine photographer Mike Brenner attached an anchor to the rear of a jacked-up Bill Bagshaw Pro Stocker. Gillespie nabbed a few pix for himself to savor the moment in December 1972.

In 1971, Billy Stepp entered the world of Pro Stock racing in a big way with a Challenger tuned by Paul Frost and driven by Stu McDade. It became a formidable foe to everyone in the Pro Stock wars. Not only did this Challenger run great, but it also won the best appearance award at both the 1971 NHRA Spring Nationals and the NHRA U.S. Nationals.

The Competitors

The Pro Stock class was showcased at the 1971 NHRA U.S. Nationals, and two of the best Mopars went head-to-head. Ronnie Sox, in the mighty Sox & Martin Mopar, got by Stu McDade, in Billy Stepp's Challenger. Stepp didn't go home empty handed, as he pulled in the "best appearing" honors.

Billy "The Kid" Stepp was considered a mobster, gangster, and notorious hoodlum. He was the most famous gangster to own a Pro Stock race car, yet he was a very nice guy to his friends and family . . . just do not get on his bad side.

One of Rufus "Brooklyn Heavy" Boyd's many race cars had problems at Englishtown, New Jersey, in 1971. Butch Leal's former Camaro broke off a wheel and needed some tender loving care.

The Dawn of Pro Stock

Chapter Three

This was a rare national event appearance for the "Brooklyn Heavy" Pro Stock Mopar at the NHRA Gatornationals, as his Pro Stock primarily match raced all up and down the East Coast. At one time, "Heavy" had a fleet of seventeen different race cars, and that was not including his "street race cars."

One thing you had to say about Rufus "Brooklyn Heavy" Boyd was that he had some of the best Pro Stock drivers in the cockpits of his race cars. The Mutt Brothers, Ronnie Lyles, Herb McCandless, and Carmen Rotunda all drove for "Heavy" and did very well on the Pro Stock match racing circuit.

To be successful in the Pro Stock class, even the privateer needed help with his car. For Jim Hayter, his help came from good friend Chuck Wright, who helped with cash and Diamond Racing engines, which supplied the power for Hayter's Camaro. Jim built the entire car himself and then jumped into the driver's seat to race. This photo was taken by Ray Mann and contributed by Quartermilestones.com.

The Dawn of Pro Stock

The Competitors

Jim Hayter traded his non-factory Camaro Pro Stock for a non-factory Vega Pro Stock when the rules changed (yet, again) to favor Vegas and Pintos. Jim mainly raced AHRA major events and match raced throughout the United States in the early to mid 1970s. John Shanks snapped this photo of Hayter at Ontario, California.

Upstart Jim Hayter gave the big factory Pro Stock a serious challenge, even though he was outmatched in the money and technology department. However, he proved he could race and beat the best in class anyway. Here, Hayter gives Ronnie Sox all he can handle at Dallas, Texas.

The Dawn of Pro Stock

Chapter Three

Dick Loehr was a fan favorite in the Funny Car class, and very popular in the Pro Stock class. Here he is showing other Pro Stock drivers how to do a fan-pleasing, tire-churning burnout. Loehr was just reaching his peak in Pro Stock when Ford cut back on sponsorships and left him out. With no sponsor, Dick sold everything and put his time and money back into his Michigan-based business, which was very successful.

DIAMOND-TOUGH IN SUFFOLK WCS COMPETITION

PRO STOCK ELIMINATOR 9.64 143.08

A DIAMOND BUILT ENGINE SETS NEW E.T. RECORD 9.67

DON CARLTON DRIVING THE MOTOWN MISSILE

Our continuous dynamometer program helps assure your continued success. Diamond Racing Engines Inc. is the place to go for all your late Hemi and big or little Chevrolet engine needs. Call or write today!

DiAMOND RACING ENGINES INC.
3493 Ten Mile Rd Warren Mich. 48091 (313) 756-4050

When the Pro Stock class exploded on the drag racing scene, the aftermarket parts people took advantage, touting the early Pro Stock stars in ads that ran in magazines and trade publications. The Motown Missile was the subject of many aftermarket ads.

One of drag racing's quickest and fastest plumbers was Atlanta, Georgia's Reid Whisnant (the other plumber in drag racing was Top Fuel racer Frank Bradley). He first started in Pro Stock in 1970 with a 1968 Hemi Dart, and by 1972 was a major contender in Pro Stock with his trademark golden Plymouth Duster.

Chapter Four

Trial and Error

The evolution of Pro Stock spread quickly in the first three full years of the eliminator class. The 1970 Pro Stock cars were basically modified Super Stock machines running 10-second times at around 138 mph, which was considered great for 1970. In 1972, the "Grumpy" Jenkins–built Vega became the first car to make extensive use of a tube-chassis frame because of the Vega's unibody construction. By 1973, the style was more akin to the *Mopar Missile*, which was state-of-the-art for the class at the time. Don Carlton's ride was considered the ultimate Pro Stock competition car, flaunting $25,000 worth of electronic recording equipment during testing sessions, which made the car a true rolling lab.

As the class progressed, Pro Stock racers started farming out chassis and major construction chores to professional race car builders, phasing out the home-built Pro Stock machines. Sox & Martin were the first to offer this turnkey service and others followed suit, offering a wide array of options to the Pro Stock racer for the right price.

Chapter Four

Ron Butler

By 1973, there were five top Pro Stock builders besides Sox & Martin in the United States. One of these was Ron Butler, who arrived in 1963 from his native New Zealand. His craftsmanship and attention to detail paid off handsomely, making him one of the premier Pro Stock competition car builders at the beginning of the Pro Stock revolution. Culver City, California, was Butler's base of operations, and this transplanted Kiwi helped build the *Motown Missile* with Dick Oldfield. He then created Butch Leal's Duster and Bill Bagshaw's Challenger, as well as Ken Van Cleave's super-trick 1973 Dodge Dart Sport.

Not only did Butler build chassis, front suspension, and rear-end components, he also had his own fiberglass front-end pieces molded. If someone wished to purchase a complete car (sans the engine and transmission) from Butler back in 1973, $16,000 was the price. That bought you one heck of a Pro Stocker.

Both Gary Kimball (left) and Kevin Rotty (right) vacated their AHRA GT-1 Camaros to go Pro Stock racing with tragic results. Kimball lost his life in a single-car crash in an ex-Jenkins Vega, and Rotty was involved in a two-car accident that took the life of Pro Stock racer Jim Trimmings.

So you think a Pro Stocker is an easy race car to drive? Think again!

Trial and Error

A couple weeks after this photo of the Millwee's Magic *racing Don Grotheer was taken, the* Millwee's Magic *'Cuda was no more. Southern California racer Geno Redd purchased the 'Cuda after this event and was killed testing his "new" Pro Stock car at Orange County International Raceway.*

Scotto & Blevins had a big year in 1972 when they won three modified eliminator titles. For 1973, Blevins debuted a new Speed Research and Development–built Chevy Vega in Pro Stock, and he soon made his mark in early Pro Stock wars.

Don Hardy

Veteran chassis and race car builder Don Hardy had his shop in Floydada, Texas. Hardy, of course, was no stranger to the building of fine drag cars. Known primarily as a funny car chassis builder, the challenge of engineering a great chassis for the new Pro Stock class called out to him. A widely known "secret" is that Sox & Martin had Hardy build all of their customer-ordered Pro Stock chassis. Don also put his craftsmanship into the Mopars of Don Grotheer and Reid Whisnant. What about Chevy Vegas? Sure—both Lee Edwards and Royce Freeman had Hardy build them. Back in the day, Hardy preferred to furnish a rolling car that the owner finished, resulting in a quicker turnover time for racers wanting a Don Hardy–built Pro Stock class car. However, Hardy didn't turn anyone down if they wanted a turnkey Pro Stocker, as it just meant more money for his effort.

Chapter Four

In 1970, NHRA debuted the Pro Stock program on its drag racing circuit, but it wasn't the only circuit to debut Pro Stock. The United Drag Racers Association (UDRA) circuit added the factory hot rods to their Midwest-based events as well. Joe Satmary quickly became the ruler of the roost in UDRA Pro Stock racing with his cast-iron 454 Chevy-powered Camaro Pro Stock car. He was a pillar of UDRA Pro Stock racing and he also ventured to other AHRA and NHRA major events. Here, John Shanks snapped a photo of Satmary at the NHRA Winternationals in Pomona, California.

Speed Research and Development

In the little town of Malvern, Pennsylvania, there was a shop that was only interested in building the best Pro Stock cars, and only Pro Stock cars. Speed Research & Development (SRD) was a joint venture between Dick Whitman, Derrick Von Bargen, and Pete Hutchinson, the master craftsmen behind SRD's Pro Stock product. After the success of the SRD-built Bill Jenkins *Grumpy's Toy* Vega, orders poured in for Vega-based Pro Stockers. The trio did a masterful job, from trimming stock components to building entire turnkey Vegas.

Scott Shafiroff, Paul Blevins, and Ray Allen all debuted new SRD-sourced Vegas in 1973. $12,000 bought a complete car with an acid-dipped body. And if you were a big spender, $28,500 got you a complete ready-to-race Pro Stock Vega. SRD knew how to build an outstanding Pro Stock. Just ask Bill Jenkins.

He was another one of those bad-ass Brooklyn, New York, street racers. "Super" John McFadden first started with a 1968 Chevy Camaro, which was modified by Dickie Harrell into an SS/AA class legal racer. McFadden then moved up to the Pro Stock class in 1971 with this Camaro and achieved cult-like status among New York street racers by racing in the most famous street race ever. For $250,000 cash, McFadden raced one of the infamous Mutt Brothers, "Rapid" Ronnie Lyles, in a winner-takes-all street race in Brooklyn, New York.

Trial and Error

Don Carlton (left) seemed a bit stunned in the 1972 Gatornationals winner's circle with Firestone Representative Bill Abraham. Carlton had just won his first NHRA Pro Stock title. Ironically, drag racing lost both men in tragic accidents: Abraham in a highway accident on his way to the 1972 NHRA U.S. Nationals, and Carlton testing his Dodge Colt at Milan, Michigan, in 1977.

Larry Huff and crew are all smiles after claiming a Pro Stock Eliminator victory at the AHRA Green Valley, Texas, Grand American Race. Huff and his Mopar Pro Stock were regulars on the NHRA and AHRA major event trail.

The Pro Stock saga of Mike Fons started with a privateer Chevy Camaro, and then the next thing we knew, he had purchased the 1972 Motown Missile 'Cuda, including the famous name. Fons later bought another car built by Kent Fuller and Dick Landy. He then purchased yet another car from Irv Beringhaus and transferred the Motown Missile name to it as well. The Rod Shop fit in somewhere, but it was all quite confusing.

The Dawn of Pro Stock

Chapter Four

Wolverine Chassis

At the home of all things automotive in the United States, only a stone's throw from the Detroit Metro airport was Wolverine Chassis. This company, owned by Tom Smith, had been building racing cars for years and was well-known in the Midwest for building funny cars. They decided to get into the Pro Stock craze in 1973. Smith can boast about building the factory Pinto of Elliot & Poole, and the independent Gapp & Roush Pinto. Smith also produced Dick Maskin's and teammate Wally Booth's American Motors Hornets. In 1973, Tom Smith built a complete race-ready car (without engine or transmission) for $16,000. Not a bad deal, both from a lead-time perspective and considering the cost, even in 1973 dollars.

Tom Smith, of Wolverine Chassis built very competitive Pro Stock race cars for Gapp & Roush. Smith also built Wally Booth and Richard Maskin's AMC Hornet Pro Stockers. Gapp & Roush ran two Wolverine-built Ford Pintos. Gapp drove one and Ken Dondero the other. Photographer John Shanks caught the Pinto during a rare West Coast appearance.

At the 1972 NHRA SuperNationals in Ontario, California, Bob Glidden and Barrie Poole clashed in the semi-finals, both in Gapp & Roush–prepped Ford Pintos. Poole ran quicker, but Glidden won on a holeshot 9.43 to a losing 9.42. It was Poole's last time at the wheel of the Pinto. He sustained injuries in a snowmobile crash and retired from drag racing. Gapp & Roush then purchased the Elliott & Poole Pinto for match racing duties in 1973.

M&S Welding

The last stop on our magical mystery tour of Pro Stock builders takes us back to California, to a little shop called M&S Welding near Los Angeles, in Azusa. There, Sherm Gunn and Mike Hoag hung their welder's helmets. They had a great little profitable business until they built a Pro Stock Maverick for "Dyno" Don Nicholson. The world exploded for the Azusa duo, with orders for Pro Stock components keeping them very busy. Being racers themselves, Mike and Sherm did all they could to help keep the cost down on any components they built.

Their shop never had the room or facilities to build full-on Pro Stock race cars. An M&S car consisted of all the fiberglass mounts, seat mounts, sheet metal, suspension, and even clutch and brake pedals positioned. There were no front fenders or hood attached. All of this was offered for $6,000 out the door. Not bad for a do-it-yourself racer.

Others

Even the hardcore Top Fuel chassis-building clan started getting into the Pro Stock revolution. Kent

Trial and Error

In 1972 in Tulsa, Oklahoma: Guardrail 1, Pro Stock Camaro 0.

Jeg Coughlin, the future high-performance mail-order guru, went Pro Stock racing in 1973. At first he drove the car, but his hands-on style of running his business required him to pass the driving duties to Jerry Miller for the second half of 1973. A second car was to be added to create a two-car Pro Stock team, but too many business dealings nixed the idea, and soon the entire Pro Stock venture was parked until almost thirty years later.

A pair of SRD-built Pro Stock Vegas went nose-to-nose at the 1973 NHRA Spring Nationals in Columbus, Ohio. A newcomer to Pro Stock, Paul Blevins took on "The Grump" in first-round action. Jenkins only qualified thirteenth in the field, but put a better-qualified Blevins on the trailer for the long tow back to New Jersey.

Chapter Four

Corky Booze was one of the few black men to compete in the early years of Pro Stock. Being from Northern California, I saw this NorCal racer move from a D/Gas 1955 Chevy, to a Super Stock AMX Javelin, to a 1969 Camaro Pro Stocker in 1970, to this Chevy Vega in 1973. Booze was a hardcore racer, but even a hardcore racer needs lots of cash to compete in Pro Stock, and he was soon priced out of the class.

Bakersfield, California–based Doug Kerhulas switched from Top Fuel to a Chevy Vega Pro Stock. Kerhulas had been seriously injured in a Top Fuel crash and, after a long recovery, he once again went racing, only this time in a Pro Stock Vega.

West Coast Funny Car racer Junior Brogden made the switch to Pro Stock with his Pee-Wee Pinto in 1973. The former Funny Car owner/driver didn't find fame and fortune in the Pro Stock ranks and soon faded.

Trial and Error

"One of a kind" is the only way to describe Roy Hill's 1973 Plymouth Duster Pro Stock car. The North Carolina self-proclaimed "hillbilly" went to the famous NASCAR racers Richard and Maurice Petty to have them build his racer. The Pettys were delighted to see what their NASCAR-style designs could accomplish on the quarter-mile. Hill went on to show that he was always a tough competitor in Pro Stock. Roy mainly raced in the IRHA and AHRA circuits, as well as the match race circuit.

Proving that Pro Stock was indeed a difficult class to compete in was former Top Gas dragster king, owner/driver Gordon "The Collector" Collett. He decided to go Pro Stock racing after the Top Gas class was dissolved. Collett didn't adapt well to Pro Stock and quickly faded away.

The Dawn of Pro Stock

Chapter Four

Fuller, Fred Forkner, and the Logghe Brothers all made contributions to the Pro Stock class. They built many of the components for the Pro Stock cars.

Another strange addition to the Pro Stock ranks was Richard Petty Engineering, which built a Mopar for Roy Hill. What is it with NASCAR going drag racing?

Innovations

Anytime you have a "stock" class, there are racers who stay true to the car being stock, and you have the renegades or innovators (depending on whom you talk to) who make changes to get a winning edge. With the introduction of the tube chassis and other innovations in Pro Stock, the cars were now quicker and faster. So, of course, that required dreaded rule changes as the NHRA rules committee considered the effects of chassis and component changes on safety.

The stock presentation of the class was upheld, including the wheelbase length, gasoline-burning engines with carburetors, and stock body dimensions and interior trim. Any changes within these basic parameters, and the class would lose its fan appeal. Aftermarket products also played into this maze of new rules, including headers, pistons, carburetors, camshafts, and many other products. They all had to fit into the Pro Stock rule-making puzzle.

The NHRA issued the new rules, and while technical enforcement at various NHRA events could be counted upon, the same could not be said at match races around the country where the rules were not enforced by NHRA representatives, but instead by more liberal track personnel.

Ultra-lightweight Pro Stock–based cars with huge-displacement (NHRA illegal) engines could still be found running all across the states, and part of the blame can be placed squarely on the shoulders of the promoters who turned a blind eye when these teams showed up in very questionable race cars. It got to the point where the legal Pro Stock racers had to match race against cars with blatantly illegal components. Reports of widespread violations of Pro Stock rules were rampant in 1973, and it caused quite a bit of concern for the true (legal) Pro Stock racers.

Shelby Jester turned the Shag Monza Pro Stocker into instant junk at Pomona, California, in 1977. The car flipped and rolled at least eighteen times at the finish line. The Don Hardy–built Monza kept Jester safe, and he crawled out of the destroyed car without a scratch, saying, "That was one e-ticket ride!" A few months earlier, Jester had done the same with the Shag Vega Pro Stock car in his home state of Texas. What fun with Pro Stocks!

Trial and Error

Larry Peternel's encounter with the Gainesville, Florida, guardrail ended with the following results: Guardrail 1, Peternel 0. Line-lock systems on Pro Stocks proved to be a bit touchy for quite a few racers.

Bert Straus traded his very popular Chilly Willy A/G Willys for a Pontiac Astre Pro Stock. An Astre-bodied Pro Stock was a rare sight in the class, and for good reason. Bert's Chief Chilly Willy Astre couldn't keep up with the Vega- or Pinto-bodied small-block Pro Stocks.

The Dawn of Pro Stock 111

Chapter Four

Photographer Norman Blake caught Bill Jenkins in full match race mode at Englishtown, New Jersey, in 1977 and 1978. Englishtown was one of many East Coast racetracks with frequent "run what ya' brung" events with much looser rules than the NHRA races. The stars of the Pro Stock circuit in full killer gear with massive cubic-inch engines, huge snorkel scoops, and wings were common at these wild Pro Stock events.

North Carolina's double-knit king, Barry Setzer, added a Pro Stock Camaro to his race team, joining Setzer's already successful Funny Car team Vega driven by veteran Pat Foster. The Camaro proved to be a disappointing venture for Setzer, resulting in a short life under the Setzer banner. It was soon replaced by a state-of-the-art Vega in Pro Stock, but that car didn't set the Pro Stock world ablaze either. Photographer John Shanks caught this image of Bruce Walker driving the Camaro.

In 1973 at Irwindale, California, a couple California boys were duking it out in Pro Stock. USC graduate Bill Bagshaw pitted his Ron Butler–built Mopar against another Butler creation owned and driven by Butch "The California Flash" Leal. Both racers had been in the Pro Stock class since its inception, with Bagshaw coming to Pro Stock from the Super Stock classes, and Leal from Stock, A/FX, and Funny Car.

The renegades were racing cars that had been modified, hoping for instant fame and a whole lot of lucrative match race bookings and cash winnings. The small group of racers who stayed true to the "stock" class found it difficult to compete against those who were cheating. Eventually, the drivers started adding language to their contracts regarding the type of car they would race, and most stated they would only race against an NHRA-legal Pro Stock car. It was clear that if NHRA didn't do something, the credibility of the Pro Stock class would be in doubt. To be quite frank, they were quickly becoming nothing but slower funny cars with doors.

The NHRA eventually imposed more stringent rules for the Pro Stock class, making it clear that member tracks would lose their sanctioning if they didn't abide by the NHRA class rules, which could dramatically affect their ability to run events. Rules were implemented to equalize competition among the brands, and everything was addressed including weight distribution, engine setback, body modification, and even overall cost. By the 1973 NHRA Spring Nationals, a lot had been ironed out by the powers-that-be at the NHRA, and they were able to save the Pro Stock class.

Safety Issues

Safety is and will always be paramount in the sport of drag racing. It was definitely a consideration in the revised rules for the new Pro Stock class. However, rules can only go so far, and even though safety considerations were applied, when the human factor is added to a very fast race car anything can happen.

The year 1974 started out on a sad note when popular Pro Stock racer Irv Beringhaus was killed in his new Don Hardy–built Ford Pinto at Scottsdale, Arizona. Irv had sold his Mopar to Mike Fons and made the switch to a small-block Ford Pinto for the 1974 season. The cage held together around the driver, but the impact was so violent that Irv's body just couldn't survive the crash. Photographer and good friend Don Gillespie shot several photos of the incident, but this one image gets the point across.

Very few Pro Stock standouts came out of the West Coast in the early days of the class. Bill Bagshaw was one of the few to impress the hardcore fans. His jump from Super Stock to Pro Stock was smooth, and things looked bright for this college-educated racer. Bill won the Pro Stock Eliminator at Lions Drag Strip's last drag race in December of 1972, but two years later he was involved in a horrific crash that killed several spectators in St. Louis. Bill tried to regroup after that accident, but in 1976 he had another bad crash and decided to retire. Bagshaw's Butler–built Mopar was caught in action by photographer John Shanks.

Chapter Four

Paul Blevins and Irv Beringhaus were a pair of rising stars in the Pro Stock class of 1973. Both of their stars faded fast when Beringhaus lost his life in a crash at the beginning of 1974 and Blevins' personal demons took him away from drag racing.

For me, Bob Lambeck was one of those unsung talented Pro Stock drivers in the early years of the class. Bob sharpened his skills driving both his and Dick Landy's Super Stock cars. When the time was right, Bob left the Landy fold and ventured out with his own Mopar in Pro Stock. Photographer John Shanks shot this photo at the NHRA Winternationals in Pomona, California.

On August 19, 1983, longtime Pro Stock racer John Hagen lost his life in a terrible high-speed crash at the NHRA Northstar Nationals in Brainerd, Minnesota. At age forty-six, Hagen had been at the wheel of his 1983 Dodge Omni Pro Stock, and his death was a great loss to drag racing. His crew chief was a young Greg Anderson (yes, that Greg Anderson) who had yet to become a star in the Pro Stock class in his Summit-backed Pro Stock Pontiac in the modern era of Pro Stock.

Unfortunately, it often does, and from 1971 to 1977, Pro Stock proved to be a deadly class.

At Orange County International Raceway (OCIR) on November 22, 1971, Geno Redd arrived to test his latest acquisition, the *Millwee's Magic* Pro Stock 'Cuda. Geno was a veteran Southern California racer with many years of experience behind the wheel of various stock-bodied race cars. The test run was straight and true until an oil seal blew, coating the rear tires in lubricant and causing Geno to lose control and strike a guardrail. The wayward 'Cuda flipped repeatedly, and Geno died at the scene.

At Thompson Drag Way in Thompson, Ohio, Harry Sinclair readied his Pro Stock Camaro to attack the quarter-mile in June 1972. It was a nice day to race, and Sinclair, a local standout who was no stranger to drag racing, made a run. It looked like a nice pass, when suddenly things went all wrong for Harry at the end of the track. He lost control and crashed violently at the 1320 mark killing another Pro Stock driver.

Irv Beringhaus began his career at the start of Pro Stock racing in 1970, when he purchased Don Grotheer's 1968 SS/AA Plymouth Barracuda and went Super Stock racing. Irv got the fever for Pro Stock racing, so he made another call to Grotheer and purchased Grotheer's 'Cuda Pro Stocker in 1971.

In 1973, he purchased a Landy/Fuller-built Duster to carry him down the 1320. At the end of the 1973 season, Beringhaus saw what the Ford Pinto faction of Pro Stock had achieved and called Don Hardy to build him a new Pinto-based Pro Stocker for 1974. Irv then debuted his all-new, Hardy-built, Gapp & Roush–powered Pinto at Scottsdale, Arizona, on January 26, 1974.

I was there as Beringhaus left the starting line and began streaking down the Arizona quarter-mile. Things went all wrong for Irv just before the finish line. There was an immense amount of dust and dirt as the Pinto began a series of flips until the wayward Pinto finally came to rest near the pit area. The Don Hardy–built Pinto roll cage/chassis had done its job holding together in this very violent crash; however, the NHRA still lost another one of its up-and-coming Pro Stock stars at the very young age of thirty-nine.

The Kimball Brothers were heavy hitters in AHRA Stock-class racing. They won many a trophy with their potent Camaro when Pro Stock came along, offering more money and more match races. At the beginning of 1973, the Kimballs purchased a slightly used Vega from Bill Jenkins and went Pro Stock racing. At an NHRA meet in Missouri on September 15, 1970, thirty-one-year-old Gary Kimball died racing the Vega, yet another victim of a violent high-speed crash.

Continued on page 121

David White walked away from this crash at Englishtown, New Jersey, in 1978. He had benefitted from all the safety innovations brought to the class by the previous generation of Pro Stock builders. Photographer Norman Blake recorded the remains of White's bent race car.

Chapter Four

Mystery Mopar? No, it was Don Carlton, who had just taken ownership of the Missile. Stewart Pomeroy purchased this car from Carlton, and Kenny Hahn drove it for Pomeroy. Why was the name changed from the Motown to the Mopar? Too much confusion with Motown Records in Detroit, or so they said. This photo was taken by Norman Blake.

It's match-race madness at Englishtown, New Jersey, in 1978 and "Dyno" Don Nicholson is taking on Bill "Grumpy" Jenkins. With both cars in full match race mode featuring big engines, big scoops, and big wings, it was time to hang on! Of course it was also Ford versus Chevy! Englishtown regular, photographer Norman Blake snapped this cool image.

"Dyno" Don Nicholson started the 1973 season by winning three consecutive national events: AHRA Winternationals, NHRA Winternationals, and NHRA Gatornationals. All saw Nicholson in the winner's circle with his 351 Cleveland-powered Ford Pinto. M&S Welding–built race cars played a big part in Nicholson's success in Pro Stock.

Trial and Error

It was Ford versus Chevy again at the 1973 Super Stock Nationals held at York US 30 in Pennsylvania. Upstart Paul Blevins put his SRD-built Vega into the winner's circle with an upset win against favored Don Nicholson. This was a big win for Pro Stock newcomer Blevins.

Modified Eliminator standout Ed Sigmon parked his Chevy-powered Opel B/A to enter the Pro Stock wars in 1973. Sigmon was reported to be driving a Ford Pinto owned by Texan Mickey Mills. Photographer John Shanks' camera made the Pinto look like a Camaro. Or is it a Camaro? Anyway, Sigmon briefly raced in Pro Stock and quickly returned to Modified Eliminator.

The saga of Kenny Hedman's Ford Maverick Pro Stock ownership was short but sad. Hedman debuted one of the state-of-the-art Pro Stockers in 1971, but luck was not on his side. He had a blown engine and then his entire rig was stolen at the NHRA U.S. Nationals. Just a shell of the car was recovered. Photographer John Shanks shot this rare photo of the bad luck Maverick.

Chapter Four

Out of Salem, Oregon, came Ken Van Cleave and his Ron Butler–built Mopar. The Mopar was said to be the lowest Pro Stock in competition. To achieve this stance, Butler engineered a dry sump oiling system to replace the low-hanging oil pan. His trick front-end pieces gave the car a ground-hugging attitude that predicted the future. This is another John Shanks photo from the 1973 NHRA Winternationals in Pomona, California.

West Coast–based Larry Breaux was a regular at Division 7 NHRA WCS races with his privateer Mopar Pro Stock. Breaux didn't have the big sponsor to tour, so he could be found racing along the West Coast. Larry was runner-up at Lions' last drag race.

118 The Dawn of Pro Stock

Trial and Error

Larry Huff was a greasy ol' drag racer before he became the Sultan of Soap. Huff added the Pro Stock class to his already successful Top Fuel and Funny Car team, but this car was different because Huff himself was driving. Huff's biggest win in his Soapy Sales Pro Stock was at the 1973 Bakersfield March Meet. His Challenger defeated the favored Bob Lambeck in the all-Mopar final round.

Larry Broga had lots of exciting moments in Bill Innes' Pro Stock Pinto at the 1974 NHRA U.S. Nationals. A failure with the line lock produced a very bent Pinto and an embarrassed driver. My buddy Norman Blake was there with his Nikon to record the action.

The Dawn of Pro Stock

Chapter Four

Virginia country boy Lee "The General" Edwards retired his well-worn Camaro Pro Stock car for a spankin'-new Don Hardy Chevy Vega in 1973. Edwards was a very well known gas coupe racer in Virginia. Lee only competed in the Pro Stock class for a couple unremarkable years.

The West Coast wasn't exactly a hotbed of Pro Stock in the 1970s. When West Coast Pro Stock racer names were mentioned, they included Landy, Leal, Bagshaw, Lambeck, and Bryant. And Lee Hunter? Well, he was a little guy in the land of giants. With a limited budget, his Ford Pinto held its own in the Pro Stock wars on the West Coast.

Lee Hunter did well enough with his Ford Pinto to trade it in for a shiny, new Ford Mustang II–based Pro Stock car. The Southern California racer was a favorite among Ford Pro Stock fans at the SoCal race tracks. Photographer John Shanks shot this image at OCIR.

Trial and Error

Two-car collisions are very rare in drag racing, and in Pro Stock in particular. When they do occur, they can be lethal for one or both drivers. Such was the case with Pro Stock racers Kevin Rotty and Jim Trimmings at Tucson Dragway in Tucson, Arizona, on October 27, 1973. Trimmings' *Underdog* Nova faced off with Rotty's Camaro. It was a clean side-by-side launch for the two Pro Stock hopefuls, when Rotty lost control of the Camaro about 500 feet out and plowed into the unsuspecting Trimmings' Nova. Both cars sustained heavy damage in the ensuing crash. While Rotty emerged unhurt, the thirty-three-year-old Trimmings was not so lucky.

Now for the Southeast's share in the carnage of the Pro Stock class: Twenty-seven-year-old Rick Metts was testing his mighty Mopar Pro Stocker at Bradenton, Florida, on March 4, 1976, when, at 100 mph, Metts slammed his Pro Stock into the guardrail, causing him to be ejected. Metts died instantly at the scene.

Then, on March 20, 1977, nineteen-year-old Tony Wood raced his 1974 Plymouth Duster at the eighth-mile track at U.S. 19 Dragway in Albany, Georgia. Tony crashed the Duster and later succumbed to his injuries, making him the youngest Pro Stock driver to die behind the wheel of one of these factory hot rods.

By far, the worst incident of the 1970s happened in St. Louis, Missouri, in 1974 when Bill Bagshaw, a popular Southern California–based Pro Stock racer, competed at the AHRA Gateway Nationals. It all happened during the first round of eliminations on Sunday, August 4, 1974.

Bagshaw ran against Texan Shane Nichols in an all-Mopar battle. Bagshaw was in the left lane when the rods kicked out and sprayed oil on the rear tires. Bill crossed behind Nichols and hit the guardrail about 900 feet down the track, broadsiding it.

Then the car made a 180-degree spin, facing the starting line. It then barrel rolled over the guardrail into the grandstand. The seats were only four rows high, and Bagshaw's Mopar simply rolled over them. As the Mopar went over the grandstand, the driver's door came open

Another person who switched from being a longtime Funny Car driver to the Pro Stock class was Texan Kelly Chadwick. He parked his very successful nitro-burning Vega for a Don Hardy–built Vega Pro Stocker. Chadwick was one of many Funny Car driver/owners to join the Pro Stock ranks, but only a lucky few were successful in the class, and Chadwick wasn't one of them. Here photographer John Shanks caught Chadwick racing Dick Maskin's Tom Smith–built Hornet X *at Indy in 1974.*

Chapter Four

Also in 1974, Malcolm "The D.C. Lip" Durham returned to his doorslammer roots with this Vega-based Pro Stocker. Durham built his Vega to match race close to his Washington, D.C., home and business. Malcolm, of course, was another of the Funny Car owner/drivers to vacate the Funny Car class and move into Pro Stock. Photographer Norman Blake took this photo of Durham and his Vega in action at Englishtown, New Jersey.

Canadian Nelson Des Champs purchased the Mr. Norm's Colt Pro Stocker and went match racing. The Dodge Colt was to be Mopar's answer to the Pinto and Vega in Pro Stock, but handling woes resulted in the car being outlawed by the NHRA. The Colt was able to race in Modified Eliminator, but not in NHRA Pro Stock. This Colt still exists today and, last I knew, it was being restored by (the late) Dick Towers. The photo was taken by Norman Blake.

To the victor go the spoils, and Paul Blevins enjoyed being in the 1973 Super Stock Nationals winner's circle. Blevins waded through a stellar field and defeated "Dyno" Don Nicholson in a Chevy-versus-Ford final. This victory in 1973 was one of the biggest in Blevins' rookie Pro Stock year.

Trial and Error

Midwesterner Paul Longenecker was there at the beginning of Pro Stock with his Chevy Camaro. But Longenecker made a bizarre switch, going from Pro Stock to a Top Fuel dragster in the early 1970s. There have only been a few driver/owners to have gone from Pro Stock to Top Fuel.

Detroit's own Mike Fons drove the team The Rod Shop flagship Pro Stocker to a 1971 NHRA Pro Stock World Championship. He also won the 1971 NHRA World Finals in Tulsa, Oklahoma, to claim the prize. In the mid 1960s, Fons was a Woodward Avenue street racer, and then in 1969 he took his 1967 Chevy Camaro to an NHRA Street Eliminator Championship. Later, he piloted his own Camaro Pro Stock car when Pro Stock came into its own in 1970. Gil Kirk and the Columbus, Ohio-based Rod Shop observed Fons' driving talent and signed him up to drive their Pro Stock entry, and the rest is history.

DRAG N

"The Drag Racer's Bible"

VOLUME 19, NUMBER 17 NOVEMBER 10, 1973 35¢

ZUL PUSHES 'RAT MOTOR' TO 8.89 E.T.

Safford Wins Miami Funny Car Championships

On October 28, 1973, Richie Zul's Pro Stock became the fastest big-block Camaro in Pro Stock with an 8.89-second pass, backed up with a 9.07 at Englishtown, New Jersey.

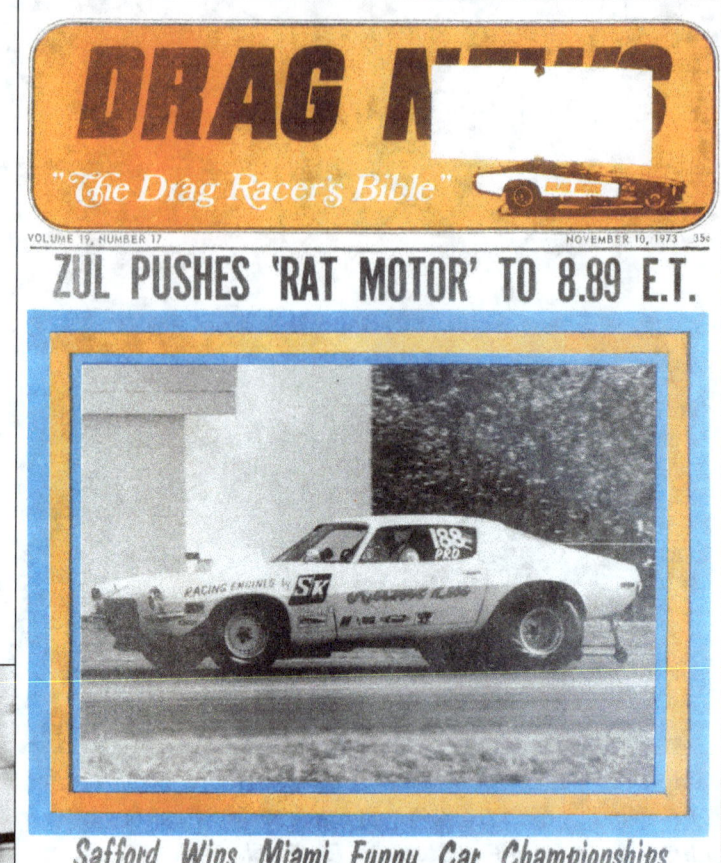

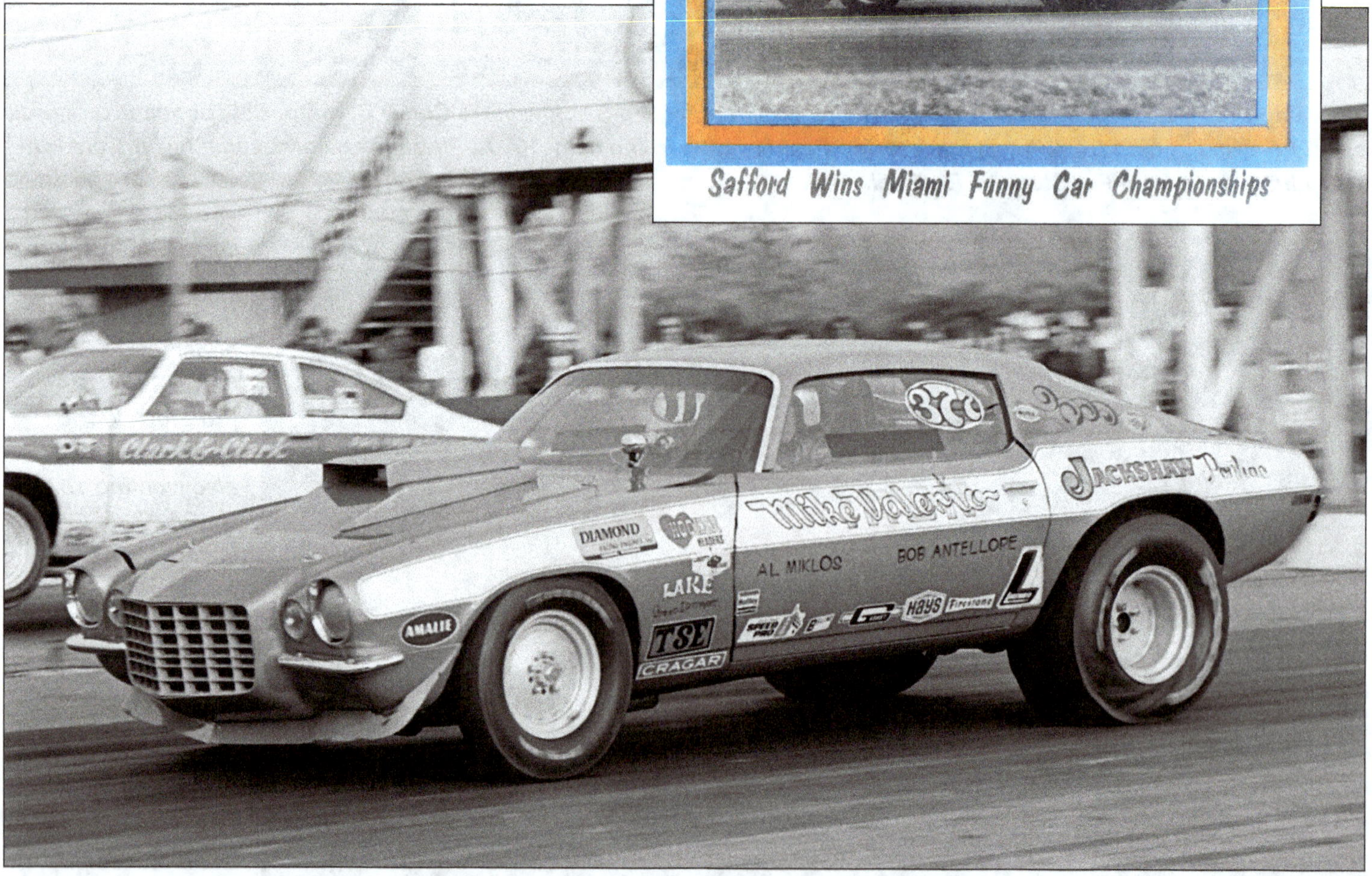

At Dragway 42 in West Salem, Ohio, Ian Landies piloted Mike Valerio's Pro Stock Camaro. "Iron" Mike's Camaro was one of the best to come out of Ohio in 1972. Valerio built his own race car with a unique, completely adjustable chassis to adapt to track conditions. "Iron" Mike also built the all-aluminum 430-ci Can Am–based Chevrolet big-block engine producing 700 hp. Valerio was the Pro Stock class' true DIY racer and he executed it well.

Trial and Error

From the gritty streets of Brooklyn, New York, came "Rapid" Ronnie Lyles, a member of the street racing Mutt Brothers along with his brother John, Eugene Coard, Benny Dunham, and Jesse Johnson. The group decided to forego street racing and enter the world of Pro Stock instead. Lyles became one of the most successful black racers in the Pro Stock class. He raced a variety of Mopar-based Pro Stockers in the 1970s.

and caught the top row. This caused a small section of the grandstand to collapse. Two spectators (Ken Myers, sixteen, of Wood River, Illinois, and Lana Reed, nineteen, of Festus, Missouri) were killed, and nineteen others were injured. A stunned Bagshaw crawled out from his Mopar. The reinforced doors provided by Butler had saved his life, but the accident had the dragstrip owners and sanctioning bodies scurrying to add new safety measures imposed by insurance companies as a result of the crash.

To this day, Bill Bagshaw does not speak of this accident. He returned to Pro Stock racing later in 1974, but then, at Irwindale, California, in 1976, he had another spectacular crash while racing Ken Dondero in a car owned by Bill Jenkins. This time when he walked away from the totaled Mopar, he also walked away from the sport he loved.

Theft

At least three Pro Stock camps suffered major thefts of race cars, trucks, trailers, and spare engines. Entering the Pro Stock wars in 1970 was Kenny Hedman with his *Hedman Hustler* Maverick, a state-of-the-art Pro Stock car debuting at the 1970 NHRA Winternationals. He entered Pro Stock racing in February, and then at the NHRA U.S. Nationals in September, the Maverick and its tow rig disappeared from its space at a local Indianapolis hotel parking lot. Hedman and the police held a frantic search for the Maverick, but to no avail. A few weeks went by, and finally the remains of the car (sans its trick Maverick body) were recovered. A very bitter Hedman never ventured back into the Pro Stock class again.

East Coast standout Richie Zul suffered the same fate as Hedman when his 1969 Camaro Pro Stocker was stolen (along with its truck and trailer) from Zul's shop. Richie found his 1969 Camaro himself, completely stripped and sitting under a bridge in New Jersey. The only thing remaining was the shell of his once mighty Pro Stocker and former street-racing Camaro. Richie's truck and trailer suffered an even worse fate, as they had been sunk in New York's East River. This was something no racer should go through, but Zul recovered, and his driving talents and engine building continued to shine in Pro Stock racing.

I saved the best (or worst) of the thefts for last, as Bill Jenkins' *Grumpy's Toy* Vega Pro Stocker and its truck were also stolen. The saga of this rip-off began August 3, 1973, on a Friday at the NHRA Gateway Nationals at St. Louis International Raceway. Jenkins unloaded his car and was quickly established as the one to beat, with an 8.97-second qualifying pass. This put him head and shoulders above the field that day. His crew loaded up the prized Vega, and away Bill and his gang went down the highway for a Saturday match race with Herb McCandless. Jenkins put McCandless on the trailer in three straight runs, and then loaded up and headed back to St. Louis for Sunday's eliminations.

Chapter Four

New York Pro Stock standout Richie Zul suffered a big-time loss with the theft of his first Pro Stocker, a 1969 Chevy Camaro. Zul located his wayward Camaro under a bridge in New Jersey, but the car had been stripped bare. The truck and trailer were also taken and had been sunk in New York's East River. Talk about a tough break!

Consider the strange case of Rick DeLisi and his Waco Kid Pro Stock. DeLisi appeared out of nowhere in Pro Stock, and then suddenly vanished. Rumors swirled about drugs, money, folks getting plastic surgery, and folks living on a boat in the ocean to escape the Feds. Lots of research later, and there is not a single person who would verify the rumors floated about Team Waco Kid. This photo was taken by John Shanks.

Trial and Error

The "Ronnies" united, with Ronnie Sox behind the wheel of Ronnie Lyles' 1974 Dodge Colt. Lyle's Sox & Martin–prepared Colt Pro Stocker was a regular on the match race circuit, and Sox often was found driving for his customer and friend Ronnie Lyles. Norman Blake shot this image of the Ron-and-Ron Colt in action.

These days, the surviving member of the Mutt Brothers, Eugene Coard, attends car shows with this restored Ron Lyles Mopar Pro Stocker. It is his tribute to his lost friends, Ron Lyles, Benny Dunham, and Jesse Johnson. If there is a car show for diabetes, you can find Eugene and the car on display. Since Lyles passed away from diabetes in 2000, Eugene attends any fundraisers that fight the disease.

The Dawn of Pro Stock

Chapter Four

On Sunday morning, the Jenkins gang went to IHOP for breakfast just a few miles from the St. Louis dragstrip, leaving the locked rig parked in front of the pancake house. After filling up on breakfast, Jenkins and his crew headed back to the rig, only to find a large empty space where the truck and trailer had been. Jenkins ventured across the parking lot to find track personnel at the hotel to see if they had moved his precious rig. It didn't take long for Jenkins to realize both his truck and race car had been stolen.

Phone calls to the local police and to the racetrack ignited a search for the stolen Vega. The track made an announcement on the PA system alerting fans that "Grumpy's" Vega had been stolen and that anyone who had seen it that morning should come to the tower and talk with the police and Jenkins about what they had seen. Seven spectators appeared at the tower, including a father with his young son.

The word was out, and the auto supply underground now had the word the Vega had been stolen. Still, there were no leads, no clues, nothing. At about 2:30 pm, a phone tip came in that for $500 Jenkins would be told where he could find his truck. Jenkins paid the $500, and he and track manager "Tiny" Meinert headed for a location at the East St. Louis rail yard. There was the truck, with spare wheels but no race car. The truck wasn't harmed at all and everything was still locked in place.

That was August 5, and even though the truck had been found with no race car, Jenkins was not too happy. Of the seven spectators who had come forward with their sightings of Jenkins' rig, one that stood out was a young boy who insisted he saw the truck, sans race car, on a dead-end farm road not far from the racetrack. The police had checked this lead at night and found nothing. Finally, on August 7, with daylight now illuminating the search area, Jenkins insisted that the local police check that area again.

That afternoon, local police and a track security man stumbled upon a farmhouse garage with Jenkins' priceless Vega inside. The race car had seen better days by this time, having been hurriedly dismembered with the engine, transmission, doors, and front clip gone. Strangely enough, Jenkins' greatest fear was losing the trick chassis and body. The partially relieved Jenkins turned his attention to getting the car ready for the $25,000 Professional Racers Organization (PRO) event in Tulsa, Oklahoma, taking place two weeks later.

Jenkins and the crew headed home to Pennsylvania to rebuild the Vega. In less than a week, Jenkins was racing at Epping, New Hampshire. He put Sox, Stu McDade, and the Gapp & Roush team on their respective trailers. Then, the Jenkins gang invaded Tulsa, Oklahoma, for the PRO race, where Jenkins defeated Butch Leal in the final to pocket the $25,000 prize, not too bad of a comeback from a near disaster in St. Louis.

No one was ever arrested for the theft of Jenkins' Vega. However, word among the racers was that a local Pro Stock racer was behind it. But, without proof, there was no arrest.

Sam Auxier's Ford Maverick Pro Stock seemed to strain to stay together at speed in 1970 at Dallas, Texas. Auxier was an early Ford Pro Stock racer who raced a line of Mustang Pro Stockers.

128   The Dawn of Pro Stock

Trial and Error

Another hardcore New York City street racer, Scott Shafiroff, parked his street-legal AHRA Super Stock and GT-1 Camaro and introduced a new 1973 Chevy Vega Pro Stock racer to the AHRA Grand American circuit. The Vega was built on an SRD chassis with a Truppi-Kling engine. Shafiroff was very serious about going head-to-head with the best in Pro Stock. Scott still builds competition engines out of Bohemia, New York, today. This photo was taken by Mike Bagnod.

Twenty-three-year-old Scott Shafiroff set out to make his mark in Pro Stock with a new SRD Vega in 1973. Shafiroff had raced a 1969 Chevy Camaro in AHRA's Super Stock and GT-1 Eliminator classes. He also could be found on the streets of New York City, winning money as one of its top street racers.

Chapter Four

In 1974, at the NHRA Winternationals in Pomona, California, Scott Shafiroff showed up with his newest addition to the Pro Stock class, a Ford Mustang II Pro Stock. He had changed out his Chevy Vega for the Ford Mustang, but unfortunately without the success that he had in 1973.

In 1972, joining the "Jungle" Jim Liberman Funny Car circus was Dutch Iragang and the Jungle Jim Vega wagon in Pro Stock. Liberman already had two Funny Cars touring, so why not a Pro Stocker too? Dutch raced the Jungle blue Vega at a few national events, but match racing was the team's bread and butter. In 1974, Liberman also added the Allison Brothers Top Fuel car to the "Jungle" Jim race team.

When it seemed as if every Pro Stock team went with the mini-bodied race car, Billy Stepp chose a Plymouth Arrow. Behind the wheel of the Pro Stock was fellow Ohioan, Bobby Yowell. Yowell wasn't the only veteran driver to make laps in Stepp's Arrow. Ronnie Sox also drove for the Dayton, Ohio, "businessman." Here, Yowell took on Bob Glidden at the Popular Hot Rodding event in Martin, Michigan.

130   The Dawn of Pro Stock

Bob Glidden raced his Ford Fairmont in 1978, 1980, and 1981. He won thirteen national event titles with his fabulous Fairmont. The folks at Ford Motor Company were truly amazed by Glidden's performance.

Chapter Five

The Four Horsemen

I guess you could say I saved the best Pro Stock owners/drivers for last. Bob Glidden, Warren Johnson, Lee Shepherd, and Frank Iaconio all had well-established records in Pro Stock racing.

Bob Glidden

One of the more productive Pro Stock owners to emerge in the 1970s was a guy from Greenwood, Indiana, named Bob Glidden. His march to fame and glory started in the 1960s with a 427-powered Ford Fairlane, which he raced on weekends after working all week as a line mechanic at his local Ford dealership, Martin Ford. Then in 1968, Glidden piloted a 428 Cobra Jet Mustang in the Stock class before moving up to Super Stock. Bob raced both classes until he got the itch to go Pro Stock racing in late 1972.

He sold his Stock and Super Stock Mustangs and went looking for a vehicle to run in Pro Stock. He found a Ford Pinto Pro Stocker being sold by the team of Gapp & Roush. The sale was made and Glidden went Pro Stock racing, only this time he decided to concentrate on his racing full time, so he quit his mechanic's job. At Glidden's first Pro Stock race, the 1972 NHRA SuperNationals

The Dawn of Pro Stock   131

Chapter Five

From 1974 to 1981, Bob Glidden won thirty-two national events and was world champion five times. He achieved his success with both Ford- and Mopar-based Pro Stockers.

Bob Glidden not only spanked the Pro Stock faithful in NHRA competition, but he managed to take the time to win an IHRA Pro Stock Championship and several IHRA events.

Glidden raced a few different Ford-bodied Pro Stockers, including a Pinto, a Fairmont, an EXP, a T-Bird, a Mustang, and a Probe. The EXP ran well, but didn't perform like the other Fords in Glidden's Pro Stock career.

The Four Horsemen

The 1973 NHRA U.S. Nationals was Glidden's first national event victory. He led the quickest ever Pro Stock field with a 9.03-second national record at 152.54 mph. Glidden defeated Gapp & Roush in the final, 9.08 to 9.09!

Glidden retired his undefeated Fairmont and switched makes at the beginning of 1979, taking on a Plymouth Arrow in Pro Stock. He started the season by winning the NHRA Winternationals and didn't lose a round of competition until June. The streak ended after fourteen races and fifty rounds when he red lit in the second round at the NHRA Mile-High Nationals in Denver, Colorado. That year he won seven national events.

At the 1980 NHRA Summernationals, Glidden took one from upstart Frank Iaconio. Glidden was the guy to beat in Pro Stock, but the New Jersey–based Iaconio was soon battling Glidden and Lee Shepherd for national event titles from coast to coast.

The Dawn of Pro Stock   133

Chapter Five

at Ontario, California, Bob was narrowly defeated by Bill Jenkins in the final round. It was obvious to all that he would be a real contender in the world of Pro Stock.

Glidden, with wife Etta and sons Rusty and Billy, now toured as a family unit from coast to coast. Etta often drove the rig, with Bob wrenching on the car while motoring to a national event or match race. How many of you have tried to work on a race car in a moving trailer? It isn't easy. All of that hard work paid off for Glidden as he scored his first national win at the NHRA U.S. Nationals in 1973. This victory was extra sweet for the Glidden clan, as the U.S. Nationals were held in Indianapolis, almost in the Gliddens' backyard. Many of their friends and fans shared in the Gliddens' victory.

Glidden's second full season running Pro Stock was in 1974, and the question of the day was whether or not the Midwest racer could ride his U.S. Nationals victory in 1973 to bigger and better things. Glidden added a win at the NHRA Spring Nationals, and then another at the NHRA U.S. Nationals. Then he claimed the big prize in 1974, the Winston Championship. He went on to win seven times in 1975 including the Winternationals, the Gatornationals, the Fall Nationals, and the World Finals. He also collected his second consecutive Winston Championship. All this was achieved with three different cars in which he qualified fifteen times, posted top speed eight times, and set low ET six times.

All the good times came to an end for Glidden during the 1976 season, with wins eluding him. He fared better in 1977, but was still short of his prior successes. However, Glidden's unrivaled work ethic put him back on top of the Pro Stock world in 1978, when he won seven national NHRA races and claimed his third Winston championship. His seven national victories broke Bill Jenkins' previous record of six, and tied Don Prudhomme for national NHRA event wins for 1978. During that winning 1978 season, Glidden used two cars, one being his Pinto, and the other his new Ford Fairmont.

Bob Glidden kept a careful eye on his wife, Etta, as she changed the spark plugs in the family's Pro Stock Fairmont at Englishtown, New Jersey.

Glidden started his second season in 1980 with his Plymouth Arrow, but when Chrysler filed for a government bailout they ended Glidden's Mopar career. The trusty ol' Fairmont was put back on the racetrack and went head-to-head with Lee Shepherd to retain his championship title.

The Four Horsemen

Glidden was number-one when he faced number-two, Frank Iaconio, at the 1981 NHRA World Finals at Ontario, California. But at the end of the race, neither were a World Champion because Lee Shepherd claimed that honor in NHRA's Pro Stock Eliminator. It was a sweet victory for Shepherd, because Glidden had edged him out in the last race of the season the year before.

The NHRA U.S. Nationals winner's circle was a very familiar place for the Glidden family. The Glidden gang celebrated victory nine times just down the road from their home base of Greenwood, Indiana.

The Dawn of Pro Stock

Chapter Five

At the beginning of 1982, Glidden's Ford T-bird was just one of the cars chasing Shepherd's Camaro. It wasn't until the middle of the 1984 season that Glidden's new T-bird was able to dominate in Pro Stock. Glidden's T-bird led the points standings from start to finish. He won five national events and his sixth Pro Stock Championship in 1985.

There were highs and lows for Glidden and Iaconio in 1984. Glidden switched to a new T-bird-based car toward the end of 1984, and this put new life in his sagging season. Iaconio, on the other hand, was not so lucky. His 1984 season was lackluster from start to finish, and he ended the year in a disappointing seventh position in the points.

During the 1979 season, Glidden retired his undefeated Fairmont for a Plymouth Arrow and yes, Ford fans, it was a Mopar product. The Arrow did not disappoint the Gliddens and brought them a victory at the NHRA Winternationals in 1979, which was a great way to start off the racing season. That mighty Mopar of Glidden's didn't lose a round of competition until June, a streak spanning more than fourteeen races and fifty rounds. Bob ended the streak himself by red lighting in the second round of the NHRA Mile-High Nationals in Denver, Colorado. At four of those events, he had set low ETs, qualified number-one, and ran the top speed. Glidden became the most dominant Pro Stock racer in the nine-year-old Pro class.

During 1980, Glidden chased Lee Shepherd all season until the World Finals in Ontario, California, where, with only a few championship points separating them, the battle was on. When Shepherd broke a transmission in the second round, Glidden won the race, again setting a low ET and the fastest MPH. That gave Glidden his third straight Winston title and his fifth overall.

Between 1981 and 1984, Glidden saw a lot more of the Texas-based Pro Stock Camaro of Reher & Morrison, with Lee Shepherd at the controls. Unfortunately for Bob, a lot of what he saw was the rear of Shepherd's Camaro as he collected Pro Stock championships from 1981 to 1984.

The Four Horsemen

When the Glidden family went on tour, they slept, ate, and worked in their rig. When traveling between races, it was common to find Etta at the wheel of the big rig and Bob in the trailer working on the race car while they moved down the road.

At the 1973 NHRA SuperNationals at Ontario, California, Bob Glidden ended Paul Blevins' hope of a victory in Pro Stock. Blevins had been Chevy's last hope in Pro Stock Eliminator that year. Glidden went on to the finals and raced Wayne Gapp. Gapp put a holeshot on Glidden and won the all-Ford Pro Stock final by running an 8.87 to a losing 8.86. It was a sweet victory for Gapp because Glidden had just defeated him a few weeks earlier at the NHRA U.S. Nationals.

At Martin, Michigan, a couple Pro Stock heavyweights did battle when Bob Glidden and his fabulous Ford Fairmont lined up against UDRA Pro Stock champ Joe Satmary and his Tuff Rabbitt Camaro. Glidden continued his winning streak with a victory against the UDRA Champion. Are you surprised?

The Dawn of Pro Stock

Chapter Five

At the 1975 NHRA U.S. Nationals, Bob Glidden was wheeling a Mustang II in Pro Stock Eliminator. Glidden changed body styles and engine combinations because of the NHRA's body, cubic-inch, and weight changes in Pro Stock. If you didn't follow the rule changes closely, you could be left in the dust on the quarter-mile. Photographer Ray Mann shot this photo.

The Pro Stock world came close to losing Bob Glidden before he was Bob Glidden the Pro Stock Champion. In 1972, during a wheel test in Bowling Green, Kentucky, a front wheel failed, sending Glidden's Pro Stock car through a guardrail. Then it clipped a telephone pole. The car, with only a roll bar and belts for safety, was torn in half. The impact not only cracked his helmet but also knocked it from his head. Glidden had recurring health problems throughout his career as a result of this accident.

The Dawn of Pro Stock

Mid-season in 1984, a new Thunderbird was delivered to Glidden. After running his new 'Bird for a few months, Glidden was ready for the 1985 season, and the only word to describe his year was "domination." From the beginning to the end of the 1985 season, he led the championship points chase and racked up five national event wins. Glidden collected his sixth Pro Stock championship for 1985.

Unfortunately, Glidden was not in championship form for the start of the 1986 season. The low point of 1986 was a wild crash at the NHRA's Southern Nationals in Atlanta, Georgia. His T-Bird was destroyed after performing six barrel rolls just past the finish line. Bob was shaken, but uninjured and most figured his 1986 season was history. However, the Pro Stock world learned you can never count Bob Glidden out. The Glidden family pulled together, and within weeks Bob returned to the Cajun Nationals with a new car. His first win of 1986 came in July at the Mile-High Nationals in Denver, Colorado. This win was the first of three straight, and he went on to win six of the final seven events for his seventh Winston Pro Stock Championship in 1986. Not a bad comeback!

Glidden was on a tear in the Pro Stock class and carried his winning well into 1987, when he proceeded to win eight national events, including his sixtieth national event victory. He ended the season with five straight wins and another Winston Pro Stock Championship. That championship was his eighth, and the Glidden family celebrated yet another championship in 1988. That was his fourth straight, and the nineteenth of his career.

Bob retired his Ford Thunderbird Pro Stocker toward the end of the 1988 season, trading it for a new Ford Probe. The Probe quickly put Bob in the winner's circle at the Fall Nationals, marking his sixty-seventh national event victory. In 1989, Glidden scored wins at five of the first seven national events, and seven of the first eleven. He won a total of nine events and took home his tenth (and final) Pro Stock Championship, drawing to a close a decade of winning that included a grand total of forty-nine national event wins.

The 1990s proved to be the final years of Bob Glidden's Pro Stock career. He won only three events in 1990, one in 1991, two in 1992, and two in 1993. Bob won his final Pro Stock event at the Mopar Nationals in 1995. The frantic pace over the years had finally worn his body down, and Bob missed much of the 1995 season due to health problems. He had open-heart surgery and did come back to race a few events in 1997. However, with all his health issues and an unhappy sponsorship arrangement, the most dominant and tenacious Pro Stock driver the class had known to date finally called it quits. Never far from the dragstrip, Glidden can still be found working as either a crew chief or engine builder for some of today's Pro Stock teams. Glidden's career was recognized by the fans of NHRA drag racing when they voted him the number-four drag racer of all time.

Warren "The Professor" Johnson

Another Pro Stock dynasty that made a name for itself was the Johnson family. Only in America could a poor Minnesota farm boy named Warren Johnson become one of the top Pro Stock racers of all time. His journey to greatness began in 1961 when he and his wife, Arlene, along with their infant son, Kurt, took their C/MP class 1957 Chevy to the races. Arlene took care of Kurt in the spectator grandstands, with Warren tending to the car and racing. During the long, cold Minnesota winters,

Talk about your Pro Stock rivalry! It's Glidden versus Warren Johnson, and it was nasty. These guys hated each other and relished any victories against each other. When asked about Warren Johnson in a post-race interview, Glidden stated, "I wouldn't give Johnson the sweat off my balls!" Clearly, Bob didn't care for "The Professor."

Chapter Five

Lee Shepherd and Warren Johnson raced each other many times between 1981 and 1984. Here, Shepherd put Johnson on the trailer at Martin, Michigan, in 1983. After Shepherd's untimely death, Warren Johnson spoke very highly of his fallen Pro Stock comrade saying, "Lee was an excellent driver who was relaxed at what he was doing; just having fun racing!"

It was war on the quarter-mile when Warren Johnson raced against Bob Glidden. These guys disliked each other with a passion. In the late 1980s and all throughout the 1990s, these two fierce competitors seriously knocked heads in NHRA Pro Stock racing.

The Four Horsemen

Warren Johnson was called on by Oldsmobile engineers in 1983 to get serious with a resurrected drag racing program for Hurst/Oldsmobile. Johnson reworked the big-block Chevrolet V-8 to create a purpose-built powerplant called the DRCE, or Drag Race Competition Engine.

After winning his first national event race in 1981 (the NHRA Summernationals), Johnson was hooked on that special feeling of success. After that first victory, Warren won at least one NHRA national event per year for twenty years in a row. It was the longest winning streak in NHRA drag racing.

The Dawn of Pro Stock

Chapter Five

the young racer concentrated on engine development. He also took night classes in engineering while working full-time in a local steel fabrication shop. All this time he toiled on his own race car in his garage behind the Johnson family home in Fridley, Minnesota. In 1971, Warren got enough cash together to go to the local Chevrolet dealership and purchase a brand-new Chevrolet Camaro. Back home in his driveway, Warren stripped the new Camaro and readied it for the newest Pro class in drag racing: Pro Stock Eliminator.

Warren put his home-built Pro Stock Camaro on his open trailer, put Arlene and Kurt in the tow truck, and headed for the 1971 NHRA U.S. Nationals in Indianapolis, Indiana. He qualified twenty-eighth in a thirty-two-car field and was one of the sixteen who lost in the first round. Through patience and persistence, Warren won his first national event eleven years later. Those years were lean ones for the Johnson family, as they learned about racing, slept in their truck at the races, and showered in friends' motel rooms. Johnson financed his racing and family life by building engines for his competitors. By 1975, Warren was not only racing his Camaro, but had also added an evil-handling short-wheelbase Vega to his entourage. This Vega and the backwoods dragstrips where he raced it gave him an education in driving Pro Stockers.

Finally, in 1975, at the age of thirty-two, Warren Johnson made the decision to become a professional drag racer. This was a make-or-break decision for him with no sponsorship and very little money, yet he was determined to conquer the NHRA Pro Stock division. With his mighty Camaro nicknamed *The Incredible Hulk*, Warren finished runner-up for the Winston Pro Stock Championship in 1976. His Camaro raced six seasons and went down the track 3,000 times. He finished fifth in the standings in 1977, and seventh in 1978.

Warren "The Professor" Johnson was still racing in 2012, even without a major sponsor. He was still running hard, just like he did since the beginning.

In 1985, at Pomona, California, "The Professor" went head-to-head with "Tricky" Rickie Smith and his factory-backed Ford T-bird. Smith became yet another in a soon-to-be long line of victims put on the trailer by Pro Stock Eliminator's resident "professor," Warren Johnson.

The Dawn of Pro Stock

The Four Horsemen

Plain and simple, Warren Johnson dominated Pro Stock in the 1990s, as he won championships in 1992, 1993, 1995, 1998, and 1999. If he didn't win, he finished second or third. He won four straight NHRA U.S. Nationals events from 1992 to 1995, and closed out the decade with another U.S. Nationals victory in 1999.

There weren't many Oldsmobile Starlite Pro Stocks, but Warren Johnson raced one for a short time. He did okay with the Starlite, but better years were ahead with many different General Motors body styles.

My first sighting of Warren Johnson was in the early 1970s when I covered a big Funny Car race at the Minnesota Dragways and he pulled up in a Pro Stock Camaro. The Camaro proceeded to do a Funny Car–style burnout, staged, and left the line pulling the front wheels, hauling butt down the Minnesota quarter-mile.

Chapter Five

He was not called "The Professor" for nothing, as Warren Johnson was a mechanical wizard and technical innovator. He introduced the Funny Car–style roll cage to Pro Stock and perfected the five-speed planetary transmission. He also prepped his own cylinder heads and intake manifolds for his engines.

From 1979 to 1981, Warren and Arlene went IHRA Pro Stock racing, where he won back-to-back IHRA Pro Stock Championships with the family's big-block Camaro that he had purchased in the early years. The Johnson family could also be found barnstorming the Pro Stock match racing circuit and, to better accommodate their racing, the family had relocated to Buford, Georgia, in 1981. Georgia had a much better climate for year-round racing and was much closer to many of the tracks in the South and Southwest. When the NHRA replaced its complex system of Pro Stock weight breaks with the straightforward 500-ci, 2,000-pound, 2,350-pound formula at the beginning of the 1982 season, Warren Johnson was back racing the NHRA events. Warren scored his first NHRA national win at the 1982 Summernationals in Englishtown, New Jersey.

The 1990s were the Warren Johnson decade in NHRA Pro Stock Eliminator, as he racked up Pro Stock Championships from 1990 to 1993, 1995, 1998, and 1999. If he wasn't winning a championship, he was second or third in points. He won 30 percent of his major events and was in the final round at 44 percent of the races. From 1992 to 1995, Warren won four consecutive NHRA U.S. Nationals. He ended the decade with six U.S. Nationals Pro Stock titles. In April 1997, he broke the 200-mph mark, and two years later, in 1999, he ran the top speed at every NHRA event.

Warren Johnson is known as "The Professor" by fellow racers and Pro Stock fans because he is a thinking man's drag racer. The NHRA described Warren Johnson as a "complex, calculating, and cerebral racer and engineer who is invariably analytical and occasionally controversial." A few innovations that fell from Warren's brain to the Pro Stock class are the funny-car-style roll cage and the perfection of the five-speed planetary transmission.

The apple doesn't fall far from the tree in the Johnson family, as son Kurt has become one of the top racers in the Pro Stock bracket. Kurt Johnson has driven his Pro Stocker to more than twenty-two NHRA event wins. For more than forty years, Arlene Johnson has held the family together through thick and thin. For the Johnson family, drag racing is a family affair even after more than five decades. NHRA fans expressed their appreciation of Warren Johnson by voting him as the seventh in a list of all-time greatest drag racers.

The Four Horsemen

It was a great start to the 1976 year for Warren Johnson's new Pro Stock career. After deciding to race full-time, Johnson finished second to Larry Lombardo (driving for Bill Jenkins) at the NHRA World Finals at Ontario, California, the last race of 1976. This photo was taken by Mike Bagnod.

During his thirty-seven years as a Pro Stock guru, Warren Johnson recorded the first 200-mph run for a Pro Stock on April 26, 1996. Then, in 1999, he made history again by running top speed at every event on his calendar. His technology innovations had set him apart from any other Pro Stock racer, period!

The Dawn of Pro Stock

Chapter Five

On May 2, 2010, the sixty-six-year-old Warren Johnson became the oldest professional winner in NHRA history as he won the NHRA Triple A Midwest Nationals in Madison, Illinois. As of May 2010, he had won NHRA's Pro Stock Championship six times and ninety-seven NHRA National events. Oh yeah, and Warren also won the IHRA Championship twice in the IHRA's Mountain Motor Pro Stock class.

Warren made the correct choice to race full-time in 1975. He finished second with his big-block Camaro in the 1976 Winston Pro Stock Championship race. The champion was decided at the last race of the season—the World Finals at Ontario, California. Larry Lombardo (driving for Bill Jenkins) beat Johnson for the prize. This photo is from the files of Quartermilestones.com.

The Four Horsemen

Lee Shepherd

The Lone Star State produced one of Pro Stock racing's brightest stars in Lee Shepherd. Like many successful Pro Stock racers, Lee started as a weekend warrior. He honed his driving skills on the Southwestern sportsman circuit. When he wasn't racing, Lee could be found on the racquetball court or at his job porting cylinder heads. His chief competitors on the sportsman circuit were a pair of University of Texas students, Buddy Morrison and David Reher. They ran a Chevy-powered Ford Maverick with Bobby Cross at the wheel.

New business ventures caused Cross to vacate the driver's seat in the Maverick. Reher and Morrison already knew who they wanted for a driver, and his name was Lee Shepherd. The shy, soft-spoken Shepherd agreed to drive the now F/G class Maverick. The trio's first big race together was at the 1974 NHRA Winternationals in Pomona, California. A victory in Modified Eliminator and the team was off and running. The Texas trio then borrowed a Corvette Stingray body and combined it with the Maverick's drivetrain, resulting in another Modified Eliminator win at the 1975 Spring Nationals. Even with their victory at the Spring Nationals it seemed as if all the sponsorships and factory support were going to Pro Stock, so the trio decided to change classes and follow the money.

From 1981 to 1984, Lee Shepherd drove the Reher & Morrison Pro Stock Camaro, and he had Glidden's number. The Texas trio captured the World Championship and became the car to beat in Pro Stock. When the NHRA switched to the 500-ci mountain motor format in 1982, it didn't hinder the Texans at all. They just kept on winning!

It was the Texas Bowtie Brigade in the winner's circle at the Popular Hot Rodding meet at Martin, Michigan. The winner's circle became a familiar place for Reher, Morrison, and Shepherd between 1981 and 1984.

The Dawn of Pro Stock

Chapter Five

In 1981, Lee Shepherd piloted the Reher & Morrison Chevy Camaro to seven victories out of eleven national events and took the Pro Stock crown home to Texas. That year also saw Glidden win three national events. The rivalry was on!

Shepherd disposed of privateer Larry Johnson at the 1980 NHRA Summernationals at Englishtown, New Jersey. In 1980, the R/M/S team collected six national event wins and three runner-ups in ten NHRA events. A broken transmission in the final race of the season prevented R/M/S from achieving its first NHRA Championship.

The year 1982 dawned with the NHRA's introduction of new Pro Stock rules. Gone were the complex weight breaks, replaced by a simple 500-ci/2,350-pound minimum formula. R/M/S's new big-block program gave them a head start on developing engines for the new generation of Pro Stock. Lee Shepherd ran a 7.86-second ET at the season opener in Pomona, California. It was the first 7-second run in Pro Stock NHRA-style racing.

The Four Horsemen

To make the plunge into Pro Stock, they hired Minnesota-based chassis builder Don Ness to build a small-block Chevy–powered Monza in 1976. Their first year in Pro Stock was almost their last when a suspension failure at speed led to an extraordinary crash at the Summernationals in Englishtown, New Jersey. A very much shaken Lee Shepherd crawled from the wreckage unhurt. However, the wreck was enough to cause Shepherd to rethink whether he wanted to be part of Pro Stock, so it was back to the sportsman classes for him. This left Reher and Morrison without a driver for the newly rebuilt Monza.

New Yorker Richie Zul left the big city and headed for the wide-open spaces of Texas to become the driver of the Reher & Morrison Monza. Meanwhile, Lee Shepherd was winning Modified Eliminator at the NHRA Cajun Nationals in 1977. The big-city guy, Zul, and the laid-back Texans, Reher and Morrison, never did gel as a team, and soon the driver's seat was vacant again. Rather than look for another driver, the team went back to Lee to try to convince him to come back and drive for them. To make the deal even sweeter, they brought a new car to the table: a Z-28 Camaro powered with a small-block engine. The Camaro's long 108-inch wheelbase was a relief for the crash-wary Shepherd, as it handled better at high speed, something the Monza never did very well.

Back on track in 1980, the Texas trio (R/M/S) and their Camaro went on a winning spree in NHRA Pro Stock Eliminator. Out of ten national events, they won six and were runner-up three times. A broken transmission during the second round of the World Finals kept them from winning the Winston Pro Stock Championship. The next year saw their success continue with six national event wins. This time the R/M/S team won the Winston Pro Stock Championship.

In 1983, Lee Shepherd became the first driver to win both the IHRA and NHRA Pro Stock Championship in the same season. He won a total of twenty-six NHRA national events in his career. Shepherd was killed in a testing accident in Ardmore, Oklahoma, in early 1985. In 2001, Lee was ranked twelfth in NHRA's Top 50 Drivers from 1951 to 2000.

Chrysler engineer and road racer Paul Gentilozzi switched to Pro Stock in 1980. At the 1980 NHRA Summernationals in Englishtown, New Jersey, Gentilozzi ran into a Pro Stock buzzsaw named Lee Shepherd. Shepherd showed him how to drive a NHRA Pro Stock and then put the Michigan-based Gentilozzi on the trailer. Paul learned his lessons well and eventually drove for "Dandy" Dick Landy.

Chapter Five

No Pro Stock team was safe when the R/M/S team was on a championship march. Here, Shepherd made quick work of Bill "Grumpy" Jenkins' Camaro at Martin, Michigan.

When asked who was the toughest driver he had ever raced, Bob Glidden responded that, without a doubt, it was Lee Shepherd and the Reher & Morrison Camaro. "He [Shepherd] did everything he was supposed to do, and it seemed like every one of us that had to run [against] him always screwed up."

The same new NHRA rules introduced in Pro Stock that helped Warren Johnson were now a help to R/M/S. The introduction of 1982's simple 500-ci/2,350-pound formula gave R/M/S a head start on their big-block program, and in developing engines for the new generation of Pro Stock Racers. At the first race with the new Pro Stock rules (the 1982 NHRA Winternationals), Shepherd cranked out a 7.86-second pass, the first 7-second Pro Stock run in NHRA history. With Pro Stock's big-block era in full swing, R/M/S was building a mountain of motors for NHRA and IHRA Pro Stock competitors. Since the NHRA and IHRA engine rules ran parallel, R/M/S now set their sights on an IHRA Pro Stock Championship.

From 1983 to 1984, Shepherd won forty-eight of fifty-four rounds of IHRA competition and won the IHRA Pro Stock Championship back-to-back. The fearsome foursome of Lee Shepherd, Bob Glidden, Warren Johnson, and Frank Iaconio accounted for every win in six seasons of NHRA Pro Stock Eliminator—a total of sixty-four races. Shepherd set the Pro Stock national ET and speed records a total of fourteen times and was honored on the *Car Craft* All Star Drag Racing Team for four straight seasons. Numerous other awards flooded in for the shy Texas Pro stock driver as well.

Life can be very, very cruel. R/M/S racing was on the fast track, with a new 20,000-square-foot shop equipped with dyno cells and several new race cars being built in Arlington, Texas. The trio had everything going the right way when disaster struck on March 11, 1985, at a test session in Ardmore, Oklahoma. Overcast weather greeted the team when they arrived at the dragstrip, which was no big deal, as Lee was only planning a couple of 60-foot blasts before loading up and heading to the Gatornationals in Gainesville, Florida. After two 60-footers, Shepherd staged and streaked down the quarter-mile.

A 7.87-second time showed on the clocks, and Shepherd hit the parachute lever and applied the brakes as he had done hundreds of times before. Only this time it was different, as a gust of wind caught the 'chute and the force was enough to lift the right front, taking the car airborne. Lee Shepherd died at the scene at forty years of age.

Shock and sadness gripped the drag racing community. Shepherd had been a friend to so many in the racing world, and his passing was especially hard to bear. Reher & Morrison had to now try to regroup. The car Shepherd had died in was put in the corner of the shop and covered.

Lee Shepherd's legacy is impressive. He reached the finals in forty-four of fifty-six NHRA national events between 1980 and 1984, winning twenty-six of them. In 1983, he became the first driver to win both the NHRA and IHRA Pro Stock Championships, and then did it again in 1984. He won every race on the NHRA tour at least once, and his NHRA record was 173–47. He was voted the twelfth top driver of all time by NHRA fans, and many people to this day still wonder "What if?"

A few years have passed since the Lee Shepherd crash. From 1973 to 1994, yours truly had traveled all across the world photographing cars and other things for Argus Publishers. During the early 1990s, I received an assignment from the flagship magazine at Argus Publishers, *Popular Hot Rodding*, to stop in Odessa, Texas, and photograph a local car collection belonging to Delmer McAfee. Delmer had started a small two-man machine shop making drill bits for oil rigs. When his workmanship was discovered by the Arabs, his business took off and he became a self-made millionaire.

Delmer and his family welcomed me like a long-lost relative and really made me feel at home. In fact, after photographing his cars, I really didn't want to leave. While there, Delmer told me what a big Pro Stock fan he had been until his favorite driver, Lee Shepherd, had died. Delmer was trying to do something in memory of his favorite driver and had been in talks with Reher and Morrison about obtaining the Camaro Shepherd had died in. Reher and Morrison were still very emotional about the accident, and really didn't want the car to leave their hands. However, Delmer wanted to put the car back to its original race-ready condition as a tribute to Shepherd.

I left Odessa and the McAfee family to continue my adventures for Argus Publishers. A good year later, I got a phone call from Delmer wanting me to photograph a special car he had just finished. It was the Reher & Morrison Camaro Pro Stocker that had been Shepherd's last ride. After a short plane ride from Los Angeles to Odessa, I met with a very excited Delmer. There, in Delmer's shop, in all its glory, was the completely restored R/M/S Pro Stock Camaro. It was like stepping back in time, as the car was flawless with every detail correct. Delmer had spared no expense with his tribute to his favored Pro Stock team. Reher and Morrison had let Delmer have the Camaro, and ol' Delmer didn't let them down. I photographed the car for Argus' *Super Chevy* magazine. It was really thoughtful of Delmer to restore the car for R/M/S, and it was my pleasure to be a part of the restoration.

Frank Iaconio

Frank Iaconio always seemed to be in the mix of a Pro Stock era dominated by Bob Glidden, Warren Johnson, Reher & Morrison, and Lee Shepherd. He won his share of national events and was a consistent finisher

Frank Iaconio and his Camaro took on Pro Stock Champ Lee Shepherd in the Reher & Morrison Camaro at the 1984 NHRA Winternationals in Pomona, California. Once again, Shepherd won the NHRA Pro Stock Championship, but sadly, it was his last.

Chapter Five

Photographer Norman Blake caught Frank Iaconio going into tricycle mode with the Iaconio & Allen Pro Stock Monza. The year was 1978 and the track was Iaconio's home track of Englishtown, New Jersey.

The Dawn of Pro Stock

The Four Horsemen

After Ray Allen sold his Pro Stocker, he and buddy Frank Iaconio teamed up to race this Chevy Monza in 1975. The Monza finally debuted at the 1976 Summernationals at Englishtown, New Jersey. Allen was supposed to be the driver, but his NHRA license had expired and Iaconio had a valid NHRA license. If the duo wanted to race, Iaconio had to do the driving chores. Photographer John Shanks snapped this image of the Iaconio & Allen Monza.

Frank Iaconio made the move to Pro Stock in 1972. Frank built a sleek, small-block-powered Vega with an SRD chassis that was very much like the Chevy favorite of Bill "Grumpy" Jenkins. Before changing to Pro Stock, Iaconio's biggest moment in drag racing was in 1969 at the Super Stock magazine Nationals in York, Pennsylvania. Besides winning the Stock Eliminator class, he took home about $10,000 in goodies with his $2,000, 1957 Chevy stocker. Photographer John Shanks took this photo of Iaconio on tour at Orange County International Raceway.

in the top four of the season-long points chase. Iaconio claimed the runner-up spot in 1979, 1982, and 1983. He began his drag racing career out of his auto repair shop in the mid 1960s, starting with a 1957 Chevy in the Stock Eliminator class, which he raced until 1970. His biggest victory was at the 1969 Super Stock Nationals at York, Pennsylvania, where he won Stock Eliminator and went home with a shiny new Mercury Cougar, other prizes, and contingency money, etc. Frank ended up winning $10,000 with a 1957 Chevy that had cost him $2,000.

In 1972, Iaconio went Pro Stock racing with a small-block Chevy in an SRO-built Vega. He raced the Vega for a couple of seasons, but things did not work out well for Frank. In 1974, he had two bad crashes that almost ended his racing career. It took him a couple of years to mend, during which time he attended to his auto repair business. One day he got together with Ray Allen, a Pro Stock racing pal who had just sold his Vega and had the itch to go racing again. The two joined forces and built a Chevy Monza–based Pro Stocker to debut at the 1976 NHRA Summernationals in Englishtown, New Jersey.

Ray Allen was to be the driver, but a last-minute problem popped up as Allen had let his NHRA license expire. If the new Monza was going to race, Iaconio was going to have to be the driver. The duo started racing hard and fast, then ventured to the NHRA U.S. Nationals at Indy and laid down 8.70s and 8.80s at a time when a 9-second run got you into any NHRA Pro Stock show. Only the elite of the Pro Stock field were cranking out 8.60s, and here were a couple of New Jersey guys running with the elite of NHRA Pro Stock racers.

The next year, the Iaconio & Allen Monza was runner-up three times and placed fourth in points in their first full year of NHRA Pro Stock racing. Since things were going pretty well, Iaconio closed up shop to be a full-time Pro Stock professional. Shortly thereafter, they picked up their first NHRA national victory at the 1978 NHRA Gatornationals in Gainesville, Florida. The team chased the Bob Glidden juggernaut the entire year, ending up third in the points race.

In 1979, they purchased a new Don Ness–built Camaro to replace a very tired Monza, which Iaconio drove to second place in NHRA points and two national event victories. For both NHRA wins, Iaconio out-dueled Bob Glidden. The following year wasn't great for the Jersey boys, as Glidden and Shepherd raked in the NHRA Pro Stock wins.

The Dawn of Pro Stock

Chapter Five

Change came in 1982 as NHRA trashed its rules for Pro Stock and mandated 500 ci for everybody's engine, as the IHRA had done since 1977. Under the new rules, Iaconio won the first race at the NHRA Winternationals against Lee Shepherd. Later that year, Iaconio claimed victory at the U.S. Nationals and placed second in points to Shepherd.

Iaconio took the big leap and became a Kenny Bernstein Ford Motorcraft team member with this Ford Thunderbird Pro Stocker at his fingertips. Iaconio raced for two years with Bernstein, during which he only collected one major NHRA event win (at the 1986 NHRA Winternationals). Bernstein then switched from Ford to Buick, and this meant the end of Pro Stock for Iaconio.

From 1972 to 1974, Iaconio raced his SRD-built Pro Stock Vega. The small-block Chevy-powered Vega also had one of the first true roll bars in a Pro Stock. Only Iaconio and Butch Leal had full roll bars in their Pro Stock race cars. Iaconio needed his twice, with two bad crashes in the Vega that left him with serious injuries, retiring him from the sport for almost two years. He only returned to driving when his then partner, Ray Allen, had an expired NHRA license and needed someone to drive their new Monza.

Then, in 1981, Ray Allen left the team to drive for Bill "Grumpy" Jenkins, and Iaconio was left as a solo act in Pro Stock racing. He captured two wins on the NHRA national circuit and ended up third in points behind Shepherd and Glidden, which wasn't bad for a privateer from New Jersey.

Then, in 1982, NHRA mandated changes to the Pro Stock Eliminator requiring everyone to run a 500-ci engine just as IHRA had since 1977. Under the new rules, Iaconio won the first 500-ci race against Lee Shepherd at the 1982 NHRA Winternationals in Pomona, California. Later in the year, Iaconio won the NHRA U.S. Nationals and ended up second in the points.

Iaconio had a banner year in 1983 and almost won the championship. In 1984, he finished seventh in the points and at the end of the year was mulling over two offers to abandon his Chevy roots and drive for the Oldsmobile or Ford factory Pro Stock teams. As fate would have it, he chose to join Kenny Bernstein's Ford/Motorcraft Budweiser team. This choice ended up haunting Iaconio until the end of his racing career. Even though he had loads of parts and money to support him, the Ford T-bird Pro Stock never lived up to its potential. It only won one national event in two years of competition, and that was the 1986 NHRA Winternationals in Pomona, California. When Bernstein switched the team to Buick, they dropped the Pro Stock effort, and Iaconio was a privateer again and free to race a GM product.

In 1988, Frank was behind the wheel of a Jerry Haas–built Pontiac Firebird Pro Stocker, which he ran through the 1989 season. With some help from Oldsmobile, he was able to change to an Oldsmobile Cutlass, which he raced to a few runner-up finishes, the last of which was at the 1993 race in Sears Point, California.

In 1995, Oldsmobile ended their racing program, thus spelling the end for Iaconio. For Frank to compete, he needed at least two million dollars, and that wasn't an amount he had in the bank. So he returned to one of his first loves in racing: building Pro Stock racing engines. Frank can now be found at his Flanders, New Jersey, shop building engines for some of the best in the Pro Stock class.

Frank Iaconio, from Flanders, New Jersey, battled Roy Hill out of High Point, North Carolina, in 1982 at Gainesville, Florida. A classic battle of Chevy versus Mopar. On this long ago day, Iaconio put the hillbilly on the trailer.

American Motors entered the Pro Stock class in a big way with the Tom Smith–built Gremlin. Wally Booth was in the driver's seat of this AMC/Smith creation, and while his wheels-up launches thrilled the fans it didn't win many races.

Afterword

Well, that wraps up the first twenty-five years of factory hot rods in the sport of drag racing. Pro Stock has proven to be a very popular class with race fans and has become a cornerstone in NHRA national events.

As this book goes to print, the racing world has lost the last of the original founders of the Pro Stock class, Bill "Grumpy" Jenkins. Fortunately, professional drag racers such as Greg Anderson, Jason Line, Allen Johnson, and Erica Enders are keeping the Pro Stock class strong for the future.

Index

A

Abraham, Bill, 105
Adam, Al, 88, 89, 93
Allen, Ray, 104, 153, 154
Allison Brothers, 130
American Hot Rod Association (AHRA), 17, 19, 20, 42, 45, 52, 61, 66, 70, 74, 91, 94, 98, 105, 109, 115, 129
    Florida Grand American, 89
    Gateway Nationals, 121
    Pro Stock Championship, 60
    Top Stock Championship, 63
    Winternationals, 42, 47, 52, 56, 66, 70, 80, 83, 93, 116
    World Championship, 45
    World Finals, 69, 70
Anderson, Greg, 114, 156
Apodaca, Larry, 14
Arons, Dick, 72, 73
Austin, Emmett "Rattlesnake," 13
Auxier, Sam, 128

B

Bagshaw, Bill, 58, 96, 102, 112, 113, 120, 121, 125
Bartush, Leonard, 93
Bat Car, 18
Baumann, John, 89, 93
Beeline Drag Way, 61
Beringhaus, Irv, 105, 113, 114, 115
Bernstein, Kenny, 154, 155
Blevins, Paul, 84, 104, 107, 114, 116, 122, 137
Bloomin' Bullet, 14
Bonner, Phil, 77
Booth, Wally, 42, 54, 71, 72, 73, 106
Booze, Corkey, 108
Bowling Green, 138
Boyd, Rufus "Brooklyn Heavy," 30, 68, 76, 92, 94, 95, 98
Bradley, Frank, 101
Brannan, Dick, 21, 24, 80
Breaux, Larry, 118
Bristol Motor Speedway, 6
Broga, Larry, 119
Brogden, Junior, 108
Brooklyn Heavy Eliminator, 94
Butler, Ron, 89, 102, 112, 113, 118

C

Cahill, Bob, 46
California Flash, 12, 69
Candies & Hughes, 7,
Capitol Race Way, 94
Car Craft, 150
Carlton, Don, 46, 53, 77, 87, 88, 89, 90, 91, 92, 101, 105, 116
Cars magazine National Championship, 42
Cars, 32
Chadwick, Kelly, 121
Charlie Horse, 25
Chevy II, 63
Chief Chilly Willy, 111
Chilly Willy, 111
Christ, Ben, 69
Christie, Dave, 76
Coard, Eugene, 125, 127
Coddington, Tom, 88, 89, 93
Collett, Gordon "The Collector," 109
Collins, Tony, 36, 59
Continental Divide Raceway, 58, 60
Coughlin, Jeg, 107
Cross, Bobby, 147

D

Dallas Raceway, 29, 30, 40, 42, 99, 128
Danekas, Marc, 22
DeLisi, Rick, 126
DeLorean, George, 81
Des Champs, Nelson, 122
Diamond Racing, 98
Dondero, Ken, 54, 82, 106, 125
Drag News, 38, 41, 49, 69, 71, 84
Drag Racing Coloring Book, 36, 59
Drag Racing USA, 6, 71
Drag-On-Lady, 24
Dragway 42, 124
Droke, Darrell, 67
Dunham, Benny, 125, 127
Durham, Malcolm "The D.C. Lip," 122

E

Edwards, Lee "The General," 103, 120
Eliminator 2, 51
Eliminator I, 51
Elliot, John, 80
Enders, Erica, 156
Englishtown, 37, 43, 57, 74, 97, 112, 115, 116, 122, 134, 144, 148, 149, 151, 153

F

Fenner Tubbs Plymouth, 16
Fisher, Joe, 76
Flashmobile, 69
Fons, Mike, 57, 92, 95, 105, 113, 123
Fontana Auto Club Speedway, 8
Forkner, Fred, 110
Foster, Pat, 112
Freeman, Royce, 72, 103
Fremont Dragstrip, 7, 12, 14, 16, 57, 67, 77
Frey, Bob, 77
Frost, Paul, 96
Fuller, Kent, 105, 106

G

Gainesville Raceway, 53, 111
Gapp & Roush, 54, 81, 82, 83, 84, 85, 106, 115, 128, 131, 132
Gapp, Wayne, 81, 84, 85, 137
Gentilozzi, Paul, 61, 149
Gilbert, Jim, 72,
Glidden, Bob, 83, 85, 130, 131–140, 148, 150, 151
Goldfinger, 22,
Green, Don, 92
Gremlin X, 72, 73
Grissom, T. W., 76
Grotheer, Don "The Okie," 62, 63, 64, 65, 66, 103, 115
Grove, Tommy, 7, 9, 20, 25
Grumpy's Toy, 37, 104, 125
Gunn, Sherm, 106

H

Haas, Jerry, 155
Hagen, John, 29, 74, 114
Hahn, Kenny, 90, 116
Half Moon Bay Dragstrip, 11, 16, 57
Hardy, Don, 65, 66, 103, 110, 113, 115, 120, 121
Harmon, Shelly, 34
Harrell, Dickie, 77
Hayter, Jim, 66, 89, 91, 98, 99
Hayward Ford, 25
Heavy Racing Enterprises, 92
Hedman Hustler, 125

Hedman, Kenny, 117, 125
Hill, Roy, 109, 110, 155
Hoag, Mike, 106
Hodges, Clyde, 88
Hoover, Tom, 93
Hornet X, 121
Hot Rod, 92, 96
Huff, Larry, 105, 119
Hunter, Lee, 70, 120
Hurley, Sam, 23
Hutchinson, Pete, 104

I

Iaconio & Allen, 153
Iaconio, Frank, 131, 132, 135, 136, 151, 152, 153, 154, 155
IHRA, 46, 109, 132, 149, 150, 154
 Pro Stock Championship, 132, 144, 146
Innes, Bill, 119
Iragang, Dutch, 130
Irwindale Raceway, 8, 112

J

Jayhawker, 19
Jenkins, Bill "Grumpy," 6, 11, 20, 26, 29, 30, 31, 32, 33, 34, 35, 36, 37, 38, 39, 43, 45, 47, 54, 63, 64, 74, 80, 82, 83, 85, 86, 87, 89, 92, 93, 94, 101, 104, 107, 111, 115, 116, 125, 128, 134, 145, 150, 155, 156
Jester, Shelby, 110
Jodauga, John, 73, 77
Johnson, Allen, 156
Johnson, Jesse, 125, 127
Johnson, Kurt, 139, 142, 144
Johnson, Warren "The Professor," 131, 139, 140, 141, 142, 143, 144, 145, 146, 150, 151
Jones, Mike, 71
Joniec, Al, 18
Jungle Jim, 130

K

Kepner, Bret, 77
Kerhulas, Doug, 108
Killen, Ron, 88, 89
Kimball, Gary, 115
King, Jake, 40, 45, 47, 76
Kirk, Gil, 68, 71, 123
Koran, Mike, 93

L

Lambeck, Bob, 59, 60, 93, 114, 119, 120
Landies, Ian, 124

Landy, "Dandy" Dick, 6, 11, 20, 28, 29, 54, 57, 58, 59, 60, 61, 105, 114, 120, 149
Landy, Mike, 58, 60
Landy's Dodge, 11, 22, 59
Larson, Bruce, 13
Law, Bo, 86
Lawton, Bill, 16
Leal, Larry Butch "The California Flash," 6, 7, 12, 14, 17, 35, 39, 58, 61, 67, 68, 69, 70, 71, 80, 94, 97, 102, 112, 120, 128, 154
Liberman, "Jungle" Jim, 10, 130
Line, Jason, 156
Lions Drag Strip, 8, 65, 96, 113, 118
Lively One, 21, 24
Lively Too, 24
Loehr, Dick, 18, 91, 98, 100
Loflin, Gene, 13
Logghe Brothers, 15, 51, 67, 110
Lombardo, Larry, 32, 145
Longenecker, Paul, 123
Lyles, "Rapid" Ronnie, 95, 98, 104, 125, 127

M

M&S Welding, 51, 106, 116
Mallicoat, Jerry, 66
Marro, Juilo, 94
Martin, Buddy, 29, 40, 47, 131
Maskin, Richard, 72, 106, 121
Matchmaker, 51
Maxwell, Dick, 46, 66, 93
Mazmanian, "Big" John, 55
McAfee, Delmer, 151
McCandless, Herb "Mr. 4 Speed," 48, 73, 74, 75, 76, 95, 98, 125
McDade, Stu, 92, 96, 97, 128
McFadden, "Super" John, 104
Meinert, "Tiny," 128
Melrose Missile, 7, 9, 20, 25, 77, 116
Metts, Rick, 121
Mid-South Super Stock Championship, 42
Milan Drag Way, 91
Miller, Jerry, 107
Mills, Mickey, 117
Milner, Dick, 19
Millwee's Magic, 103, 115
Minnesota Dragways, 143
Mopar Missile, 77, 89, 90, 101, 116
Mopar Nationals, 139
Mortimer, Gale, 69

Motown Missile, 53, 88, 89, 93, 100, 102, 105
Mr. Norm's, 122
Mutt Brothers, 98, 104, 125, 127
Myers, Ken, 125

N

National Challenge, 74
National Dragster, 49
NASCAR, 42, 81, 82, 84, 85, 109, 110
 Winter Championship, 42
National Hot Rod Association (NHRA), 10, 12, 15, 16, 17, 24, 27, 29, 31, 33, 36, 41, 42, 45, 49, 46, 52, 55, 57, 63, 66, 67, 70, 71, 73, 77, 80, 83, 84, 85, 90, 91, 104, 110, 112, 113, 115, 122, 132, 135, 140, 141, 142, 144, 147, 148, 149, 150, 151, 153, 154, 155, 156
 Cajun Nationals, 71
 Central Division Top Stock Points Championship, 63
 Division 4 Championship, 63
 Fall Nationals, 134
 Gateway Nationals, 125
 Gatornationals, 52, 56, 66, 76, 84, 90, 92, 98, 105, 116, 134, 153
 Grand Nationals, 69, 70, 71
 Mile-High Nationals, 132, 136, 139
 Nationals, 85
 Northstar Nationals, 114
 Pro Stock Championship, 151
 Southern Nationals, 71, 139
 Spring Nationals, 29, 30, 52, 63, 71, 72, 73, 77, 96, 107, 113, 134, 147
 Summernationals, 34, 37, 39, 43, 52, 66, 71, 74, 132, 141, 148, 149, 153
 SuperNationals, 41, 106, 131, 137
 Triple A Midwest Nationals, 146
 U.S. Nationals, 31, 35, 49, 52, 65, 66, 72, 73, 80, 81, 96, 97, 105, 117, 119, 125, 133, 134, 135, 137, 138, 142, 143, 144, 154, 155
 Winston Finals, 71
 Winston Pro Stock Championship, 52, 134, 142, 146
 Winternationals, 6, 33, 39, 40, 42, 43, 49, 51, 56, 63, 64, 72, 76, 80, 90, 92, 104, 114, 116, 118, 130, 132, 134, 136, 147, 150, 151, 154, 155
 World Finals, 84

World Championships, 6, 16, 45, 52, 123, 134, 135, 136, 145
Ness, Don, 153
Nichols, Shane, 121
Nicholson, "Dyno" Don, 6, 8, 11, 13, 15, 17, 20, 29, 37, 49, 50, 51, 52, 53, 54, 55, 56, 67, 77, 80, 82, 89, 90, 106, 116, 117, 122

O

Old Reliable, 31, 86
Oldfield, Dick, 88, 89, 93, 102
Olympics of Drag Racing, 42
Ontario Motor Speedway, 51, 98, 134, 135, 136, 137, 145
Orange County International Raceway, 34, 71, 103, 115, 120, 153

P

Paper Tiger, 11, 42
Pappas, Joe, 88
Parks, Wally, 40
Paul Harvey Ford, 80
Payne, Randy, 80
Pee-Wee, 108
Penetration, 14
Peternel, Larry, 111
Petty, Maurice, 109
Petty, Richard, 109, 110
Platt, Hubert "The Mouth of the South," 6, 8, 16, 26, 62, 77, 78, 79, 80
Pomeroy, Stewart, 90
Pomona Raceway, 26, 32, 37, 40, 44 49, 52, 58, 63, 66, 90, 93, 104, 114, 118, 130, 142, 147, 148, 151, 155
Poole & Elliot, 80, 85, 106
Poole, Barrie, 80, 81, 85
Popular Hot Rodding, 80, 88, 130, 147, 151
Professional Racers Organization, 94, 128
Proffitt, Hayden, 10,
Prudhomme, Don, 134

Q

Quarter Horse, 25

R

Rat Pack, 42
Redd, Geno, 103, 115
Reed, Lana, 125
Reher & Morrison, 136, 147, 148, 149, 150, 151
Richard Petty Engineering, 110
Ritchey, Les, 8, 9

Riverside Raceway, 28
Ronda, Gas, 22
Rotty, Kevin, 102, 121
Rotunda, Carmen, 94, 95, 98
Roush, Jack, 84, 85

S

Satmary, Joe, 137
Schartman, Edward "Fast Eddie," 13, 17
Schumacher, Don, 69
Scottsdale, see "Beeline Dragway"
Sears Point, 155
Setzer, Barry, 112
Shafiroff, Scott, 104, 129, 130
Shag, 110
Shahan, Shirley, 7, 14, 15, 23, 24, 68
Shepherd, Lee, 131, 132, 134, 135, 136, 140, 147, 148, 149, 150, 151, 154
Sigmon, Ed, 117
Sinclair, Harry, 115
Smith, "Tricky" Rickie, 142
Smith, Ammon R., 87
Smith, Joe, 16, 66
Smith, Tom, 106, 121
Snorkasaurus IV, 28
Soapy Sales, 119
Sox & Martin, 11, 29, 40, 41, 42, 43, 44, 45, 46, 47, 48, 66, 73, 74, 76, 94, 97, 101, 102, 103, 127
Sox, David, 48
Sox, Ronnie, 6, 11, 20, 29, 31, 40, 41, 42, 43, 44, 47, 48, 70, 73, 77, 80, 85, 89, 91, 92, 98, 127, 128, 130
Sparks, Tom, 63
Speed Research & Development (SRD), 33, 104, 107, 117, 129, 154
Speher, Ted, 88, 89, 93
St. Louis International Raceway, 125
Stampede, 18, 91
Stardust, 69
Stepp, Billy "The Kid," 46, 76, 77, 83, 92, 93, 94, 96, 97, 130
Stone, Woods & Cook, 57
Straus, Bert, 111
Strickler, Dave, 9, 15, 20, 31, 36, 85, 86, 87
Studio Dodge, 16
Super Chevy, 151
Super Stock, 153

T

Talmadge, Pete, 74

Terry, Ed, 25
Tharpe, Richard, 6
The Incredible Hulk, 142
The Rod Shop, 57, 68, 90, 105, 123
Thompson Drag Way, 115
Thompson, Mickey, 7, 8, 67, 69
Tijuana Taxi, 84,
Trimmings, Jim, 102, 121
Truppi-Kling, 129
Tucson Dragway,
Tuff Rabbitt, 137
Tulsa Raceway Park, 16, 74, 94, 107, 123, 128

U

USA-1, 14
U.S. 131 Dragway, 50, 51
U.S. 19 Dragway, 121
U.S. Open Championship, 42
Underdog, 121
United Drag Racers Association (UDRA), 104, 137

V

Valerio, "Iron" Mike, 124
Van Cleave, Ken, 102, 118
Vanke, "Akron" Arlen, 6, 20, 52, 64, 72, 73, 91, 93, 95, 96
Vaughn, Linda, 70
Veleska, Bob, 91
Von Bargen, Derrick, 104

W

Waco Kid, 126
Wade, Earl, 50, 52
Wale, Joe "Q-Ball," 19
West Palm Beach, 89
Wetton, Jim, 16
Whisnant, Reid, 101, 103
White, David, 115
Whitman, Dick, 104
Wolverine Chassis, 106
Wood, Tony, 121
Wright, Chuck, 98

Y

York US 30 Dragway, 55, 87, 117
Yother, Cecil, 25,
Yow, Melvin, 76, 77, 83, 90, 92
Yowell, Bobby, 92, 130
Yuill, Brad, 61

Z

Zul, Richie, 49, 81, 125, 126, 149

Additional books that may interest you...

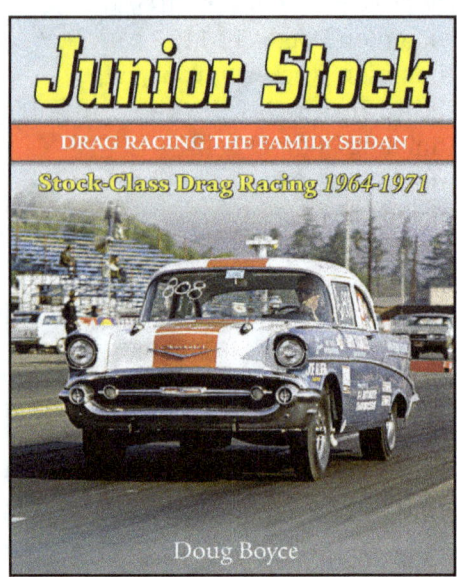

JUNIOR STOCK: DRAG RACING THE FAMILY SEDAN *by Doug Boyce* In the 1950s and 1960s, drag racing was an exciting new sport that anyone with a car could participate in. Based on their equipment, the participants' cars were assigned to specific classes. This class format encouraged amateur participation on a level never before seen. Stock-class drag racing is celebrated in this book, with hundreds of vintage color photographs showing the way it used to be. If you were a fan or participant back in the day, or are a lover of vintage drag cars, *Junior Stock: Drag Racing the Family Sedan* is a book you are sure to thoroughly enjoy. Softbound, 8.5 x 11 inches, 176 pages, 458 color photos. **Item #CT505**

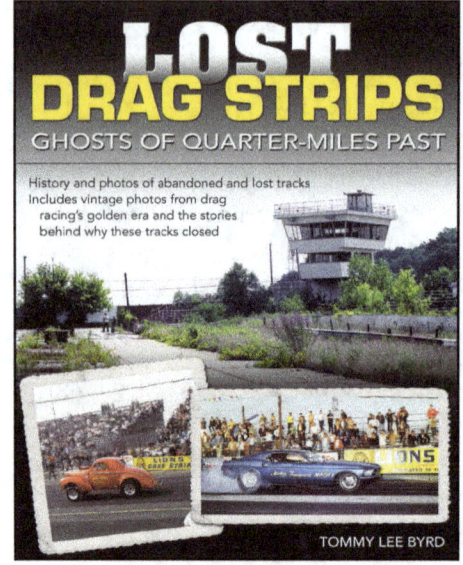

LOST DRAG STRIPS: Ghosts of Quarter-Miles Past *by Tommy Lee Byrd* This book takes a look at many of the lost quarter-mile tracks across the country. Some of them are gone completely, paved over to make room for housing developments or strip malls. Others are ghostly remnants of what once was, offering a sad and even eerie subject for the photographer. The images are teamed with vintage shots of drag racing's glory days, sharing what once was one of America's most popular pastimes with the modern reality facing these facilities today. For fans of drag racing's past, it's a sobering and interesting study. Softbound, 8.5 x 11 inches, 176 pages, 315 color and b&w photos. **Item #CT514**

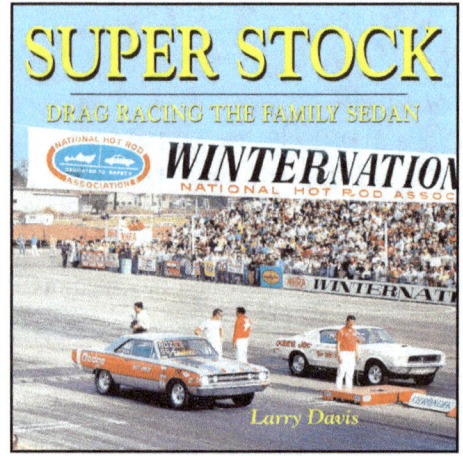

SUPER STOCK: Drag Racing the Family Sedan *by Larry Davis* This book traces the evolution of the cars, the engines, the rules, the personalities, and many of the teams, from its beginnings in the mid 50s through to the 60s and the era of the Super Stock 409s, Ramchargers, 421 Pontiacs, and 406 Fords. This was a time when Ford, Chrysler, and General Motors competed on a weekly basis at local drag strips throughout the country, and the saying "Win on Sunday, sell on Monday" had real significance in the marketplace. The hardcover best seller is gone, but now you can get it in paperback. Softbound, 9 x 9 inches, 210 pages, 310 color & b/w photos. **Item # CT495**

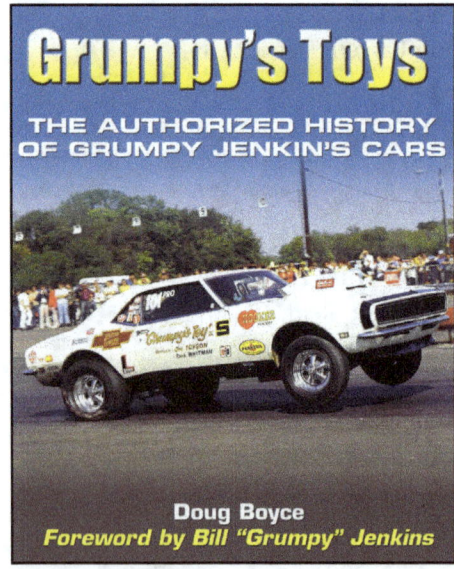

GRUMPY'S TOYS: The Authorized History of Grumpy Jenkins' Cars *by Doug Boyce* This book follows Jenkins' career through the cars he developed. This fascinating introspective showcases the innovation and record-setting performances of the many competition vehicles he worked on, including his long line of personal cars. The stories behind all of Grumpy's legendary *Toys* are here, but so are the tales and truths about the many other cars, teams, and drivers Jenkins has worked with (and against) in his five decades as one of the premier engine masters in drag racing's history. Author Doug Boyce has invested countless hours in researching Jenkins' career, and spent time with the man himself to verify all the information he acquired. Softbound, 8.5 x 11 inches, 176 pages, 300 photos. **Item # CT489**

Check out our new website:

CarTechBooks.com

✓ Find our newest books before anyone else

✓ Get weekly tech tips from our experts

✓ Get your ride or project featured on our homepage!

Exclusive Promotions and Giveaways on Facebook Like us to WIN! Facebook.com/CarTechBooks

www.cartechbooks.com or 1-800-551-4754

www.ingramcontent.com/pod-product-compliance
Lightning Source LLC
Chambersburg PA
CBHW051410070526
44584CB00023B/3364